The Little
Digital
Camera Book

Cynthia L. Baron and]

Peachpit Press • Berkeley, (

D1511257

The Little Digital Camera Book

Cynthia L. Baron and Daniel Peck

Peachpit Press

1249 Eighth Street
Berkeley, CA 94710
(510) 524-2178
(800) 283-9444
(510) 524-2221 (fax)

Find us on the World Wide Web at: www.peachpit.com
To report errors, please send a note to errata@peachpit.com
Peachpit Press is a division of Pearson Education

Editor: Becky Morgan
Production Coordinator: Lisa Brazieal
Copyeditor: Sally Zahner
Compositor: Christi Payne
Indexer: Rebecca Plunket
Cover design: John Tollet with Mimi Heft
Cover illustration: Bud Peen

ISBN 0-321-12530-4
9 8 7 6 5 4 3 2 1
Printed and bound in the United States of America.

Dedications

To my husband Shai, for making every day worth a shot

To my dear friend Nancy Bernard, for lightening my load

To Dan, my terrific partner and buddy

—Cyndi

Sarah, my one and only, for love and forbearance at any distance, and a great eye

Cyndi, my forever friend and partner

David Gahr, Diane Arbus, Edward Curtis, Walker Evans and all of my photographic heroes who used technology to reflect the world and create art

—Dan

Acknowledgments

Cyndi:

Thanks and appreciation to Becky Morgan, our editor at Peachpit, for being in our corner.

Big hugs and thankyou's to Rushika, Maria, the children and their friends.

A hearty thank you to the March 16th gang: Mary & Werner Hampl, Irene & Mike Shea, John & Karen Czaban and Jane & Tom Fama, for being willing Canon-fodder.

Dan:

Our beloved editor Becky Morgan.

Nancy Ruenzel and Marjorie Baer at Peachpit for everything.

Sarah Boslaugh and Kaitlyn MacCalla for their wonderful photos.

Sarah Boslaugh, Brad, Sheila, Megan and Kaitlyn MacCalla, Denise Lambusta, Adam Engst, Betty Vornbrock, Billy Cornette, Phil Levy, Steve Mason, Dale Morris, Sofia Tsinis, Yuliya Shapirshteyn, and Veronica Bakhrakh for their patient modeling.

Mayn chaver Paul Leichter at Tristate Camera for *klung eytse* and *ale mohl a git gesheft*.

Laurie Platt-Winfrey and Fay Yap-Torres at Carousel Research for tireless photo research.

Kirsten Odegard for luring me away from silver halide.

Chaco Canyon, Mesa Verde, Canyon DeChellys, Dinehtah and Ruckersville, Virginia for their exquisite beauty.

Table of Contents

Chapter 1 What Is Digital Photography?   3

A Brief History of Photography 2
How Film Photography Works 3
Inside a Digital Camera 4
    Film Photography Advantages 5
How Digital Photography Differs 6
    Digital Photography Advantages 7
Preparing Your Computer 8
    RAM 9
    Storage 10
    USB 10
    CD Recorder 12

Chapter 2 Buy Your Camera Gear   13

Resolution and Megapixels 13
    1 Megapixel 14
    2 Megapixels 14
    3 Megapixels 14
    4+ Megapixels 14
Optical vs. Digital Zoom 15
Auto and Manual Modes 15
Price Comparison Shopping 16
    Basic (under $500) 16
    Deluxe ($500 to $800) 16
    Professional (over $800) 17
    Mail Order 17
    Retail Store 18

Comparing Battery Types 18
   Batteries 18
   Battery Packs 20
   Adapters 20
Comparing Storage Media 20
   SmartMedia 21
   CompactFlash 21
   Memory Stick 22
   Card Readers 22
Do You Need the Extras? 23
   Camera Bags 23
   Lenses 23
   Filters 24
   Tripods 24
   Odd and Ends 25

Chapter 3 Compose a Good Photo   27

Setting Up a Shot 27
Framing the Shot 29
   Avoiding Framing Problems (Parallax) 30
Choosing the Optimum Distance 32
   Determining What's in Focus 33
Working with the Light 34
   Gauging the Light Source 35
   Shooting Against the Light 36
F-Stop and Shutter Speed 38
Shooting Motion 39

Chapter 4 Set the Camera Options   43

Resolution 43
   Choosing the Right Resolution for Your Purpose 43
   Setting Resolution on the Camera 44
Focus 44
   Using Autofocus 46
   Using Manual Focus 47
   Using Macro Focus 47
Exposure 47
   What Does Autoexposure Do? 48
   Setting Shutter Priority 48

Setting Aperture Priority 49

Using Manual Exposure 49

Setting Exposure Compensation 50

Setting White Balance 50

Zoom 51

Using Optical Zoom 52

Using Digital Zoom 52

Flash 52

Reducing Red Eye 53

Using the Flash to Fill In Light 53

Shooting without the Flash 54

Shooting at Night 54

Flash Correction 55

Self-Timer/Remote Control 57

Chapter 5 Store and Transfer Your Photos   59

Choose Your Images 59

Viewing Stored Images 60

Deleting an Unwanted Shot 61

Connect to Your Computer 61

Connecting Directly to Your Computer 62

Connecting a Card Reader to Your Computer 63

Organize Your Computer for Images 64

Transfer Your Photos 64

Transferring Photos from Flash Card to Computer 64

Transferring Photos with Infrared Connection 66

Erasing Your Flash Card 66

Swapping Flash Cards 67

View Your Transferred Photos 68

Viewing Your Photos on a Computer 68

Viewing Your Photos on a TV 70

Save and Organize Photos 70

Renaming Transferred Photos 71

Saving Your Originals 71

Organizing Your Photos 72

Burning a CD of Your Images 73

Recording Your Images on a VCR 74

Organize with iPhoto 74

Chapter 6 Choosing Editing Software 77

Why Do You Need Software? 77
Choosing Software 78
    Freeware and Shareware vs. Commercial Software . . . 79
Types of Editing Software 80
    Drop and Crop 84
    Image Editors 86
    Freeware Image Editors 88
    Commercial Image Editors 90
    Photo Editors 92
    Professional Editing Software 94

Chapter 7 Photos and File Types 95

Choosing an Image File Type 95
    JPEG 96
    TIFF 98
    RAW 98
    System File Types 100
    Web Graphics Formats 100
    Proprietary File Formats 101
Changing an Image File Format 102
    TIFF Options 104
    JPEG Options 105
    Quality 105
    Standard or Optimized Options 107
    Progressive Option 107

Chapter 8 Image-Editing Basics 109

Knowing What to Fix 109
Image-Editing Tools 111
    Selection Tools 112
    Red-Eye Reduction 112
    Hue, Contrast, and Brightness 114
    Levels 117
    Curves 119
    Dodge and Burn 119
    Layers 120
    Masks 123
    Cloning 124

Cropping 126
Sharpening 127
Changing Resolution and Size 130
Changing Print Resolution and Size 130
Changing Image Resolution and Size 132
Proportions and Aspect Ratio 133
Final Touches 134
Adding a Border 134
Adding a Caption 135

Chapter 9 Improve Your Photos   137

Fixing Brightness and Contrast 138
Using Brightness and Contrast Sliders 138
Using Levels 140
Correcting Color Shifts 141
Using Hue/Saturation 141
Using Levels 142
Altering and Editing Images 144
Making People Look Better 144
Erasing Large Objects 148
Creating a Mask 151

Chapter 10 Print Your Images   153

Why Print at Home? 153
Inkjet Printers and Cartridges 154
General-Purpose vs. Photo 155
Types of Cartridges 157
Maintaining Your Printer 159
Choosing Your Paper 160
Paper Types 160
Special Papers 162
Setting Up Your Image 164
Printing Several Images on One Page 164
Having Professionals Do It 167
Local Printing Services 168
Online Photo Printing Services 169
Uploading and Ordering Photos 170
Prints from iPhoto 171
iPhoto Printed Albums 173

Chapter 11 Share Your Photos   175

Sharing without a Computer 175
Emailing Your Images 177
  Preparing a File for Emailing 177
  Why do you need compression? 178
  Compressing files 179
  Attaching an Image to Email 180
  Sending and receiving attachments in AOL 181
Online Photo Services 181
  Using Photo Service Pages 182
  Selecting an Online Service 183
  Using iPhoto to Share Online 185
  Creating a Personal Web Page 186
Displaying Photos on PDAs 187
Making a Digital Slide Show 188

Chapter 12 Photo Projects   191

Make a Picture T-Shirt 191
Create Photo Greeting Cards 193
Make a Photo Panorama 194
Use Your Photos for Auctions 197
Customize Your Computer Desktop 198
  Create Desktop Backgrounds 198
  Create Your Own Screensaver 201
Shoot Movies with Your Camera 203
  Make a Movie with iPhoto 204
Add Sound to Your Images 205

Appendix A Digital Camera Troubleshooting   207

Appendix B Image Editing Troubleshooting   211

Appendix C Online Resources   215

Index   219

What Is Digital Photography?

The last ten years have seen a revolution in photography. Not since the advent of the Kodak Brownie camera at the beginning of the 20th century has there been such a technological advance in picture taking. Although digital cameras have been available for over a decade, they were until recently far too expensive and complex for anyone but professionals. But, just as the Brownie made photography affordable to almost anyone, recent advances have brought the price of digital cameras down to as low as $100. A digital camera allows you to shoot a picture, view it immediately, transfer it directly to a computer—and from there you can print it, post it on a Web page, or send it to friend. No more buying film or visiting the drugstore to have it processed. And the camera is just as easy to use as your trusty Kodak Instamatic. Maybe easier.

A Brief History of Photography

The history of photography can actually be dated as far back as classical Greece, when it was noted that a box with a small hole on one side produced an image on the inside of the opposite wall. Of course, there was no way to record the image, so it was a curious optical trick with no practical application. In the 16th century, Italian artists used this effect to construct the *camera obscura*. This "camera" was a small hut with a hole in one wall. It produced an image on the opposite wall, where an artist could hang a sheet of paper and trace the projected image.

Although further refinements like the glass lens, which created a sharper image, were developed to make the projected image more accurate and the device more portable, it wasn't until the 19th century that chemists worked out a way to make a permanent image. Certain chemicals reacted to exposure to light, and by coating paper or a glass plate with a solution of silver salts and then exposing it to light through a lens, a permanent image could be recorded.

For the next century, photography evolved, but it remained the province of professionals and dedicated amateurs. The process of making a photograph was complex, requiring noxious chemicals and quite a bit of equipment. The cameras were large and the length of time the film had to be exposed to light to record an image was measured in hours and minutes.

But at the beginning of the 20th century, the real fun began. The technology matured to the point where photographs could be taken with only a fraction of a second of exposure. That combined with more accurate chemical processes meant that a good photograph could be obtained with a small handheld camera like the Brownie. This put picture taking in the hands of anyone who could point the camera and press a button. The camera still had to be returned to the manufacturer to have the film developed and prints made, but that was a small price to pay for pictures of your kids. The later proliferation of processing labs further reduced the wait time. Still not instant gratification, but better.

In the 1950s, Polaroid introduced cameras that produced a print directly from the camera. Although the quality of a Polaroid was not on a par with a traditional photograph, the immediacy outweighed the quality for many people.

Which brings us to the subject of this book. The digital technology revolution of the last 20 years has produced cameras that can record visual images without using chemicals. A digital camera employs electronic sensors that record light as a digital computer file. You can view that file instantly and then transfer it to a computer where you can edit the images, email them to others, display them on the Web, or print them to paper.

When digital cameras first reached the market, they were expensive and they required a certain amount of expertise to use. (Sound familiar?) But in the last five years, digital cameras have gotten cheaper and easier to use. And with the evolution of the quality of the recorded image, a camera that can produce a good-looking photograph can be had for about the same price as a film camera. So we now have the digital equivalent of the Brownie. And you don't have to shell out for film.

How Film Photography Works

The film in a standard camera is a roll of plastic that has been coated with a gel (called the *emulsion*) that contains microscopic grains of silver halide spread evenly through the emulsion. The silver halide reacts when exposed to light.

This reaction is revealed when the film is soaked in a chemical (the *developer*), which turns the specks of silver halide dark where the light was brightest. This process produces a *nega-*

tive, which can then be used to print a positive image (a *print*). (The process works in reverse on film that produces a positive image—such as slide film.) The picture results from the varying reaction of the specks. The areas of the film that received the most light will have the highest density of dark specks; areas that got the least light will have the lowest.

Color film has three layers of emulsion. Each of these layers has a dye that lets only red, green, or blue light through to the film. Since all visible colors are combinations of red, green, and blue light, the varying levels of exposure from each layer, overlaid on each other, results in a full-color image.

Film photography records an image by focusing the light coming through the camera lens onto the film. The camera controls how much light reaches the film by using a shutter. The *shutter* is like a door between the lens and the film. The proper amount of light is determined by the shutter speed (how long the door stays open) and the *aperture* (how wide the door opens). In Chapter 3, we will discuss how that combination affects what a photograph looks like.

Inside a Digital Camera

The workings of a digital camera are not that different from a film camera's. From the outside, both cameras appear pretty much the same. There's a lens to point at your subject and a shutter button to press when you take your picture.

But inside is where the difference lies. In the place of film, the digital camera has a small plate that is covered with a grid of light sensors. The sensors are referred to as *pixels* (short for *picture element*). You may be familiar with pixels on the computer. They represent the smallest element on a computer display, and are the unit of measurement for screen resolution. The most basic digital camera has about a million pixels (known as a *megapixel*). Better cameras have several million. The more sensors, the finer the detail you can record, and the larger the image that you can print.

Each of these sensors has a filter that lets in red, green, or blue light, like the dyes on color film. Each pixel records the varying amounts of color at that point in the image.

When you press the shutter button, the camera records the amount of each color that each pixel sees. The camera's micro-processor, like the one that runs a computer, assembles the color information in a digital file and saves the file to a stor-age device in the camera. You can then transfer the resulting file to a computer, where a graphics program can reconstruct the millions of little pieces of red, green, and blue data into a visual image.

Film Photography Advantages

Despite the revolutionary advances in digital-photo technol-ogy, there are still some things a film camera can do better than a digital camera. Although many of these advantages aren't that big a deal for everyday snapshots, you should still take them into consideration.

- **Resolution**

    The *resolution* (the level of detail) of a film image is higher than that of most digital cameras. Large prints (*blow ups*) can be created from film without a significant loss of quality. The size and quality of prints made from digital images is limited by the resolution of the camera. We will discuss this in detail in Chapter 4.

- **Shutter Latency**

    A film camera records its image the instant you press the shutter button. A digital camera takes a couple of seconds to process an image and save it. So there can be a delay of a second or two between the time you press the button and the when the camera actually records the image. In technical terms, this is referred to as *shutter latency*. When you are shooting action shots like a sports event or kids playing, you may not get the picture you thought you were getting. Since you can't take another picture until the process is complete, you can't usually shoot a fast sequence of pictures. (Some digital cameras do offer features that overcome this limitation.)

- **Capacity**

    Another more subtle consideration is storage capacity. Digital cameras store photographs on one of several forms of storage cards. These cards have a finite capacity. Once a card is full, you must delete shots, have another card available, or transfer the pictures to a computer so you can safely erase the card. With a film camera, you just pop in another roll. The price of storage cards continues to fall, but they are still more expensive than a roll of film. So if you will be using your camera where you don't have access to a computer, you must invest in extra storage cards.

- **Batteries**

All modern film cameras use batteries to power the electronics that handle automatic exposure and focus. Because these chores do not use a great deal of power, the battery can last months or longer before wearing out. Digital cameras, on the other hand, use battery power to do everything—so battery life is measured in hours. You'll use a lot more batteries with a digital camera than with a film one. This puts you on a short tether if you are going to be away from a source of electricity for any amount of time. You'll either have to carry lots of extra batteries or plug in somewhere on a regular basis. So if you're hiking the Appalachian Trail, you might be better off with a film camera.

- **Cost**

The price of a quality film camera is lower than its digital equivalent. This is especially true for a full-fledged 35mm camera with interchangeable lenses. Currently the cost of prints from film is lower than from digital cameras, though that difference is getting smaller. And while you'll never have to buy film for a digital camera, you'll probably have to invest in storage cards and batteries.

How Digital Photography Differs

A digital camera offers some remarkable advantages over film photography. The immediacy of seeing your pictures on the spot alone may be enough to outweigh the disadvantages. But there are many other reasons to make the jump from film.

Digital Photography Advantages

- **Immediacy**

The majority of digital cameras have a built-in screen, so you can see the picture you just took as soon as you take it. You will never again have to wonder if a shot came out right.

- **Usability**

You can transfer your pictures to your computer directly from the camera, eliminating the need for a scanner (and its inherent distortions). So you could take a picture, transfer to the computer, and send it to a friend in a matter of minutes.

- **Reusability**

Digital cameras use storage cards to save pictures. After you transfer your work to a computer, you can delete the shots from the card and start over. So you will never have to buy film or have it processed.

- **Duplication**

A film camera produces a picture as either a negative for print making or a positive for use as a slide. If the original is lost or damaged, so is the picture. A digital image can be copied many times and not lose quality. And like your computer data, it can be backed up.

- **Adaptability**

Once you have taken a digital image, you can use it in many ways. You can save a high-quality version for printing and make a lower-resolution copy for use on a Web page or in email, all from the same image. You can do the same with scans of film images, but scanning introduces distortions and loss of quality. And scanning photos is time consuming to say the least.

- **Flexibility**

Most digital cameras have settings that allow you to easily compensate for different lighting situations. For instance, you can set the camera to automatically get rid of the reddish cast that shows up in pictures taken with incandescent light. You can adjust the flash settings to take pictures at night without losing the background. Although these features are sometimes available on film cameras, a digital camera allows you to immediately see the results.

- **Size**

A film camera has to be constructed to allow for the size of the roll of film. So even the smallest aren't that small. Digital cameras don't have this limitation, so they can be made smaller and in different shapes (**Figure 1.1**). This also allows manufacturers to create cameras with swivel lenses, so you can take a picture of a subject that is not directly in front of the camera.

Figure 1.1 Dan loves his Nikon FM dearly, but he can fit the Olympus 510 digicam in his shirt pocket.

Preparing Your Computer

You might think that having a computer is the first prerequisite for using a digital camera. Although it makes many things a lot easier, it is not an absolute essential. You can take your camera or storage card to most photo labs and have them print the images or convert them to a CD (compact disc) for permanent storage. You can also use the photo kiosks that are now appearing in malls and stores to create prints. Just plug your storage card in, view the photos on a TV screen, choose the ones you want, and produce prints right there.

But since you probably do have a computer, your horizons are considerably broadened. You can use your computer to sort through your photos, deleting the ones you don't like and organizing the keepers. You can also edit your pictures, cropping out things you don't want, lightening or darkening, and other tricks that used to be accomplished only with some work in the darkroom.

In the next chapter, we will review in detail the accessories—like storage cards and computer cables—that you will likely need to get the most from your digital camera.

If you purchased your computer in the last few years, it is probably capable of handling the tasks required to work with your digital camera. If it is older, it may still meet your needs. As a rule, any computer that is rated at a speed of 300 MHz or more will do a reasonably good job of image editing.

Most digital cameras ship with software for both Windows and Macintosh. Before you buy a digital camera, check the requirements for the included software. (See Chapter 6 for more about software and system requirements.) If you are going to be doing much image editing, the faster your computer is, the more you're going to enjoy using your camera with it. With the price of memory (RAM) and storage (hard drives and CD recorders) at an all-time low, it's not difficult or expensive to turn your computer into a photo editor.

Although software is nearly always included with a digital camera, you will not always have to use it. Many cameras can plug into a USB connector on your computer and transfer pictures without adding any software to your computer. If you already have your own editing software, you are not constrained by the included programs.

RAM

The more memory (RAM) your computer has, the easier it will be to work with your digital photographs. Exactly how much you need depends on the type of editing you want to do and how you plan to use your photos, but you can never have too much memory. 128 MB is the minimum we recommend. If you are going to do any serious retouching or other editing of your photos, 256 MB would be better.

With the price of RAM constantly dropping, adding it will not require a huge investment and will pay dividends. Plus, RAM is usually one of the easiest things to install in your computer. Most owner's manuals give step-by-step instructions on what type of RAM to buy for your computer, and how to insert it into its slots.

Storage

Depending on the resolution you used when you shot the picture, a single digital photograph can take up anywhere from a few kilobytes of space on your hard drive for a low-quality, Web-only photo to several megabytes of space on your hard drive for a nice 4 x 6-inch color print. As you continue to add more pictures, they will quickly fill up even a good-sized drive. Image-editing software may also demand a fair amount of free space on the hard drive. If you don't have at least one gigabyte of free space on your drive, you might want to consider upgrading your hard drive, or adding a second one to your computer. (Many computers have a second connection and an extra space for another hard drive.) At current prices, a new 80 GB internal hard drive will cost less than $200—much less if it will be your second hard drive and you won't be using it to run applications as well.

If upgrading your hard drive is not an option, removable storage devices like Zip drives can be used to take the strain off your system. Some computers allow you to easily add external hard drives.

Keep in mind that a floppy drive, which can store only about 1 MB of data, will not be of much value for storing your photos. You would only be able to fit a couple of medium-quality digital photos on a single floppy disk.

USB

Universal Serial Bus (USB) is the most commonly used method for transferring pictures from a digital camera to a computer. Most current computers ship with USB ports, as have all Apple Macintosh computers since the original iMac, as well as most name-brand PCs for the last two years. USB ports (on the right, next page) usually in the back of your computer with all the other ports and connectors.

  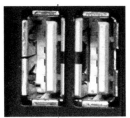

If your computer doesn't have a USB port, you can often install an expansion card in your computer to add it. Adding expansion cards requires taking your computer apart, which is easier to do with some computers than it is with others. If you run screaming at the sight of a socket wrench (or don't know what a socket wrench looks like), you should leave the installation to your computer dealer).

You can plug many cameras into the USB port and transfer the photos directly onto the hard drive or other storage devices. If you have USB ports but are using them for other things (like a Palm), you can get a USB hub that allows you to attach multiple devices to the same port. If you only have a standard serial port and can't add USB, there are inexpensive adapters available for USB compatibility. The transfer rate of photos over a serial port with an adapter tends to be pretty slow, so if this is your only option, you might want to consider using a card reader, which has a higher transfer rate, instead of directly connecting (see Chapter 5 for more information on these options).

If your computer is running Windows 95, Windows NT, or a Mac operating system (OS) version earlier than 8.5, you will have to upgrade the OS, since none of these support USB.

If your computer has a FireWire port (also known as a iLink or IEEE -1394), you can use it to easily add external drives. FireWire is similar to USB, but it transfers data considerably faster. It is commonly used to connect digital video cameras to a computer.

CD Recorder

One solution to the problem of your hard drive filling up with digital photos is a CD recorder, often referred to as a *burner*. You can store up to 675 MB of pictures on a single CD at the cost of less than a dollar. You may already have a CD burner in your computer if you bought it within the last couple of years. Note that CD burners and CD players look a lot alike, but they are not the same thing. Although a CD burner can also play CDs, a CD player can't make a new CD. Check your owner's manual if you're not sure what your computer has.

If you decide to buy a CD burner, you'll find lots of inexpensive options. If you'll just be using the burner to store photos, you can get a very inexpensive but not very fast CD burner (around $120) that you can plug into one of your computer's USB ports. If you plan on using the same CD burner for music and video as well, you should probably consider something faster.

Remember that burning photos to a CD will not just save you hard drive space. It just gives you a great medium to inexpensively send photos to friends, relatives, and even customers (**Figure 1.2**).

Figure 1.2 A CD recorder provides easy permanent storage for your digital masterpieces.

Buy Your Camera Gear

Your first step when you get into digital photography is buying your camera. And in so doing, you'll inevitably find yourself navigating a vast landscape of jargon: *megapixels, digital zoom, U.S. warranty, accessories not included*. It's enough to make you want to remain safely in the film world. This chapter will help you learn the language and understand what you need to get started.

Resolution and Megapixels

The *resolution* of a digital camera refers to the amount of detail the camera records when you take a picture. It's expressed in *megapixels*, which is a measurement of the number of sensors the camera uses to record the picture. The more megapixels, the better the picture and the more things you can do with it. But the importance of a camera's resolution depends on the kinds of pictures you want. If you use a picture as part of a Web page or to make a small print, you won't see much difference between a top-of-the-line camera and a basic consumer model. If, on the other hand, you make a large print, the difference will be all too obvious (**Figure 2.1**).

Some cameras advertise an "effective" megapixel count. This means that they are using the electronics of the camera to estimate the effect of more pixels. This does not work very well. Always use the actual pixel count when comparing models.

Figure 2.1 This picture looks pretty good at its original size. When enlarged, the lack of detail in the original begins to show.

1 Megapixel

Although 1-megapixel cameras are still available, they aren't usually a good choice. Unless you're on a severely limited budget or you only want to use the camera to post pictures of your ukulele collection on eBay, we don't recommend investing in such a limited camera. For not much more, you can get a 2-megapixel camera that will yield noticeably better pictures.

2 Megapixels

For most purposes, 2-megapixel cameras offer the best trade-off between price and quality. You'll be able to make prints up to 5 x 7 inches with good results. If you want pictures for Web pages or email, 2 megapixels will more than do the job.

3 Megapixels

With 3-megapixel cameras, you can make prints as large as 8 x 10 inches. The level of recorded detail begins to approach that of film. If you plan more demanding uses of your camera, you should consider a camera in this range.

4+ Megapixels

At 4 megapixels and beyond, you enter the realm of the professional. For most purposes, the extra detail won't be very noticeable. But if your plans include taking pictures that you will want to enlarge to any great degree, the increased resolution will make a difference.

Optical vs. Digital Zoom

The zoom on a camera allows you to make the subject appear closer to the camera without actually moving closer. When this is accomplished by adjusting the lens (*focal length* in photographic lingo) it is known as *optical zoom*. When it is done by the camera's electronic circuitry, it's known as *digital zoom*. In simple terms, optical zoom is good; digital zoom, not so good.

Optical zoom is better because it records the image at full resolution, so you get a sharp image at any level of zoom. Digital zoom, on the other hand, creates the effect of zooming by enlarging a portion of the image, just like you could do on your computer. But this results in a lower-resolution image (**Figure 2.2**).

Zoom levels are measured as 2X or 3X. A 2X zoom will let you make the subject appear up to twice as close. A 3X zoom will, not surprisingly, make the subject appear three times as close.

Figure 2.2 At maximum optical zoom (top), the skyline is clear and sharp. Although digital zoom brings the skyline closer (bottom), the details are less sharp.

Some inexpensive cameras don't have optical zoom. As this is limiting, you should strongly consider models with 2X or 3X optical zoom.

Auto and Manual Modes

All cameras offer an automatic exposure setting. The camera determines how much light is coming in and sets the exposure accordingly. Some cameras also give you the ability to set the exposure manually. If you want that kind of control, say for handling tricky lighting situations, night shots, or special effects, you'll want this feature. Many cameras include preset auto settings, specifically for night shots, bright sunlight, and other common shooting situations. These presets give you the best of both worlds—good control without your having to know exactly how to do it.

Most cameras have autofocus. This allows you to specify (usually by aiming at your subject while holding the shutter button) exactly what you want the camera to focus on. You'll use this setting for the majority of your shots. Some less expensive cameras have fixed focus. This means that everything from a few feet to infinity will be in focus when you take a picture. But you'll have no control if you want to take a shot with the focus set at a particular distance. You'll find this particularly limiting when you want to get a close-up. Some cameras have manual focus in addition to autofocus. Manual focus lets you specify the focus distance. If you are an advanced photographer and want that kind of control, opt for this feature.

Price Comparison Shopping

Now that some of digital photography's technical terms have been defined, you're ready to see what's available. The first question you have to answer when shopping for anything is "How much do I want to spend?" Digital cameras are available for as little as a hundred dollars and as much as several thousand.

Basic (under $500)

If you're going to use your digital camera for snapshots, such as family photos and vacation pictures, this is likely to be your price range. The resolution of cameras in this range will be 2 to 3 megapixels. You'll get quality pictures suitable for posting to a Web page or emailing to relatives, and prints of up to 4 x 6 (the size of a standard print from the drugstore). You probably won't get advanced features like manual control, but you can count on automatic exposure and focus, optical zoom, and preset controls for indoor/outdoor lighting.

Deluxe ($500 to $800)

If you want the control that a traditional 35mm film camera gives you, like manual exposure and focus control, this is the price range to consider. You'll get at least 4 megapixels of resolution, so enlargements up to 8 x 10 will still look good. Additional features will often include the ability to record sound and short videos, external flash capability, larger storage capacity, and the ability to add telephoto or wide-angle lens adapters.

Professional (over $800)

Once you get beyond $800, you enter the realm of the professional. Resolution will be 5 megapixels or higher. Features will cover just about anything you're likely to want or need, like remote control, continuous shooting, and a broader array of auto and manual settings for exposure and white balance. Also in this range are the 35mm digital cameras with interchangeable lenses and a wide variety of accessories. The 35mm type of camera will likely set you back several thousand dollars, so it remains the province of the professional or the wealthy.

When you've decided what your price range is, it's time to go shopping. Your choices generally boil down to either mail order/online or retail store.

Mail Order

If you're confident of your abilities and don't need any hand-holding after your purchase, online or mail order could be your best choice. A simple Web search for the name of a camera model will yield thousands of results, including technical details and a dizzying array of prices and purchase options. Prices will generally be lower than if you bought from a retail store, but you'll be on your own if you have questions or problems before or after the sale. See the appendix for a list of Web sites where you can compare features and prices.

If you go the online or mail-order route, take the phrase *caveat emptor* to heart. Most online/mail-order dealers are honest and provide good customer service. But if the one you choose doesn't deliver an acceptable level of service, you may find it difficult to resolve problems. Be especially wary if the price offered is significantly lower than other dealers' prices. Make sure before you buy that all accessories are included and that the camera has a warranty that's valid where you live. Keep in mind that the advertised price doesn't usually include shipping and handling, which is likely to be a *lot* more than you'd expect.

When ordering online or by phone, always use a credit card. If a problem arises, you'll have more recourse than if you paid by check or money order.

Retail Store

If you want guidance about what to purchase or a resource for help after you've bought your camera, a good local store is the best choice. A store that specializes in cameras will offer the most informed advice and better after-sale support. The price may be higher than with mail order, but that disadvantage is offset by greater expertise and a more liberal return policy. If you want a lower price but don't want to go the mail-order route, you can also look at local electronics superstores or even discount chains like Wal-Mart. Either way, a retail store also gives you the chance to actually touch and play with various models before you buy. No matter which way you decide to go, make a point to pick up and feel a camera before you purchase it. Getting a good sense of weight and ease of use may save you the frustration of a bad choice.

Dealers nearly always want you to buy an extended warranty. For an extra sum, this extends the period during which you can have your camera repaired without having to pay for it. Most cameras on the market today, however, are quite reliable. If they work out of the box, they are likely to work for a long time. As a rule, we don't recommend paying for repairs that you probably won't need.

Comparing Battery Types

Batteries are the lifeblood of a digital camera. And you'll be using lots of them. Digital cameras offer two choices for batteries: rechargeable lithium and either standard or rechargeable AA.

Batteries

- **Lithium**

  Lithium batteries have the longest life between charges. The type that recharges in the camera is handiest, since you don't need an external charger. But if you're going to be away from a source of AC for long periods, you'll need to carry extra batteries. Lithium batteries are harder to find outside of camera stores than AA batteries, and they're considerably more expensive (usually $30 and up).

If your camera uses AA batteries, you have more options.

- **Alkaline**

Alkaline batteries are the most common and least expensive type of standard batteries. However, they are not rechargeable, so when they are played out, you have to buy more.

- **NiCad**

NiCad (nickel cadmium) batteries are more expensive than alkalines, but they can be recharged. The disadvantage of NiCads is that they don't last as long between charges as alkalines do before needing replacement. NiCads can only be recharged 50 times or so, and they should be run down completely before recharging to avoid shortening the life of the battery.

- **NiMH**

NiMH (nickel–metal hydride) batteries offer the bestboth worlds: They last as long as alkalines but are rechargeable. The one drawback is price. They cost as much as $3 per battery and require a special type of charger. Since they can be recharged hundreds of times, though, they are a worthwhile investment (**Figure 2.3**).

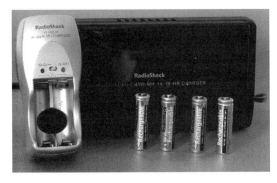

Figure 2.3 NiMH batteries are a significant investment, but they pay off in the long run and are environmentally responsible.

NiMH, lithium, and NiCad batteries should not be tossed in the trash when their life is over. The heavy metals they contain are a source of environmental contamination. Check with your local waste authority for the proper place to dispose of them.

Battery Packs

If you will be making great demands on batteries, there are a couple of options you might consider. Some cameras (usually the type that take AA batteries) will use non-rechargeable lithium batteries. These will last longer than any of the types listed above, but they are just solid waste once they go dead—they can't be resurrected by recharging.

Some cameras can use an external battery pack. It usually plugs in where the AC adapter goes and will power the camera for many hours. But since these packs are an extra item outside the camera, they aren't always convenient to use.

Adapters

If your camera uses rechargeable lithium batteries, it will include an AC adapter. To recharge the batteries, you plug the camera into an outlet via the AC adapter and wait a few hours. If your camera uses AA batteries, you may have to buy an AC adapter separately. You probably won't be able to use the camera as a recharger. Most cameras will operate without batteries if plugged into a AC outlet (with an adapter), but some models may require a different adapter than the one that recharges the batteries.

Comparing Storage Media

The storage medium is the digital equivalent of film. Some early digital cameras used computer floppy disks for storage; you could pop the disk out of the camera and into your floppy drive to transfer the shots. But floppy disks hold a measly 1 megabyte (MB) of data—not much in this day and age. Sony made some cameras that used a type of rewritable compact disc. Like the floppy models, you could put this disc into a drive on your computer and see your work. But it took along time to write each picture to the hard disk, so you had a longer wait between shots. And it was murder on battery life.

Virtually all current digital cameras use solid-state storage devices, usually referred to as storage cards. These use no moving parts to record, so they are much more reliable than the floppy or CD models, and they use less battery power. Plus, they record shots quickly, minimizing the wait time.

Today's market offers three types of storage cards: SmartMedia, CompactFlash, and Memory Sticks. Capacities range from 8 MB to 256 MB. Most cameras include an 8 MB or 16 MB card, but you'll want to buy extra, usually larger capacity, cards. Prices (ranging from $20 to $60) for all three types are about the same.

SmartMedia

SmartMedia cards are wafer thin, are about two inches square, and are available in capacities from 4 MB to 256 MB. The disadvantage of SmartMedia cards is that the contacts are exposed. If you get dirt or fingerprints on the contacts, the camera may not be able to read the card. Rubbing the exposed area with a pencil eraser will usually solve the problem, but this vulnerability is something to consider (**Figure 2.4**).

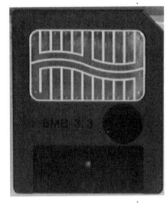

Figure 2.4 SmartMedia cards are the thinnest and lightest type of storage cards.

CompactFlash

The most widely used form of storage card is the Compact-Flash (**Figure 2.5**). It's a bit thicker than a SmartMedia card and runs from 4 MB to 256 MB in capacity. Unlike SmartMedia cards, the contacts on a CompactFlash card are not exposed, so they are less susceptible to damage from handling. If your camera accepts Type II Flash cards (thicker than its sibling, the more common Type I), you can get a card that uses a tiny hard drive (the SuperDrive) with a capacity of a gigabyte (1 GB equals 1000 MB). Check the camera specs to see if it accepts Type II cards.

Figure 2.5 CompactFlash cards are used in half of all digital cameras on the market.

Figure 2.6 If you have a Sony camera, you'll be using the Memory Stick.

Memory Stick

Memory Sticks are used exclusively with Sony cameras (**Figure 2.6**). Memory Sticks are about the size of a stick of gum and come in the same range of capacities as the other cards.

Card Readers

Even though your camera can attach directly to your computer to transfer your photos, this method is often slow and inconvenient, not to mention a waste of batteries. A *card reader* is a device that uses a serial port or a Universal Serial Bus (USB) port for quick transfer of data from your storage card to the computer (**Figure 2.7**). You remove the card from the camera and insert it in the reader, and the card appears on your computer as if it were a drive. You can then copy the photos onto your hard drive. Many card readers handle several types of storage cards, which is useful if you own more than one camera. At a cost of less than $60, a card reader is a worthy investment.

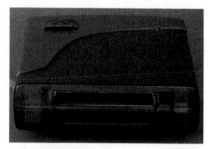

Figure 2.7 This USB card reader will accept both SmartMedia and CompactFlash cards.

*If you'll be using your camera with a laptop computer, there are card readers that fit in the PC Card slot. This convenient solution lets you avoid carrying around an extra piece of equipment (**Figure 2.8**).*

Figure 2.8 If your laptop has a PC Card slot, an inexpensive card reader will do the job.

Do You Need the Extras?

Depending on your needs and ambitions, you may have to add some items to your digital camera arsenal. Of the items listed below, only the camera bag is a true necessity. The rest meet particular needs; any one of them might be just the thing you need to perfect your photos and enhance your digital-photography experience.

Camera Bags

Since you have made a significant investment in your digital camera, it makes sense to invest a few dollars more in keeping it safe and sound. A good camera bag will protect your investment from the elements, not to mention nasty bumps. Bags range in size from small ones that can clip to your belt up to full backpack sizes that can hold your lunch or even your laptop. Look for a bag with good padding and enough room for batteries, storage cards, and other accessories (**Figure 2.9**).

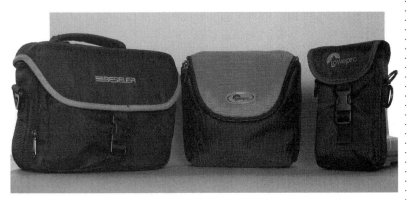

Figure 2.9 A good camera bag is both a convenience and essential protection for your expensive equipment.

Lenses

Some digital cameras allow you to use a lens adapter. A lens adapter attaches to the front of the existing lens, usually by screwing in. You can get adapters that bring the subject closer (telephoto) or pull back to cover a wider area (wide-angle). Lens adapters unfortunately introduce distortions in your pictures, so you might want to try one out before committing your hard-earned bucks. You may find that many cameras don't even offer different types of lenses. For instance, you won't find screw-on lenses for a "clamshell" camera that tucks its lens back into the camera body when you shut it off, since you'd never be able to close the camera with the additional lens in place.

Filters

Filters are a common tool in film photography. A filter can create a starburst look or filter out certain types of light for different effects. Since many of these tasks can be accomplished with software, the use of filters in digital photography is less common. If your camera has a threaded lens, as with the adapters above, you can use filters. If your camera does accept filters, get an inexpensive neutral filter. This will not affect the look of your photos, but it's good protection for the lens. It's cheaper to replace a couple dollars' worth of filter than a lens.

Tripods

A tripod provides a stable base for your camera while you're shooting. This allows you to precisely line up a shot, which is handy when you create a panoramic shot (see Chapter 12). If you're shooting in low light and don't want to use the flash, a tripod will hold the camera steady enough to get a clear shot at a slow shutter speed. A tripod will also allow you to actually be in a picture that you take, using either the timer feature or a remote control, if your camera has one. A table tripod is a small version that's easy to carry around and that serves most of the same purposes (**Figure 2.10**).

Figure 2.10 A table tripod has many of the advantages of a full-size tripod, but you can put it in your camera bag.

A *monopod* is a single leg support that steadies the camera for long exposures (**Figure 2.11**). Monopods are great for places like museums, where you might want to shoot a low light picture without flash.

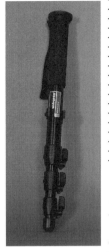

Figure 2.11 A monopod is a more portable alternative to a tripod, but it won't stand up on its own.

Odd and Ends

As with any possession, digital cameras will happily absorb as much money as you're willing to throw at them. The paraphernalia varies greatly in terms of both price and value—some items are indispensable, others are just cool, and some are both!

Additional Flash Cards

One of the first accessories you buy will undoubtedly be extra storage cards. The card that comes with your camera will probably not have enough capacity to be useful. Keep it as a backup and get yourself a 64 MB or 128 MB card—you'll be glad you did. If you travel away from your computer for extended periods, get several.

Lens Cleaner

Because a digital camera lens is smaller than its 35mm counterpart, smudges and dirt on the lens will be more noticeable in your photos. If it's not included with your camera, get a lens cleaning kit (liquid and wipes) and a brush to get rid of dirt.

Never use paper products to wipe your lens. Scratches are forever. To prevent scratches, always brush off dirt before using a lens wipe to remove the smudges.

Volume Storage

If you're not the type to schlep a computer along on your vacation, you may need a way to transfer pictures from the storage card so you can go out and take more pictures. A device like the Digital Wallet (www.mindsatwork.net) provides storage capacities from 3 GB to 20 GB, for $300 to $450. It's about the size of a book; you plug your storage card into it to transfer the shots to its internal hard drive until you get back to your computer. The Wallet doesn't let you view the pictures, but if you're going to be doing a lot of shooting and you don't have a fistful of extra storage cards, you might look into this option.

Digital Album

If you really want to feel like you're living in the future, look for a *digital album* or *digital frame*. With a digital frame, you can load your photos and have the display change automatically at intervals. Digital albums like the Nixvue (www.nixvue.com) function like the Digital Wallet, but have an output that connects to a TV to view the shots you've transferred to it. These are quite expensive at the moment, but if you're into way cool stuff, this qualifies.

Compose a Good Photo

Even if you pay a lot of money for a digital camera, it won't automatically take good pictures for you. You'll have to help it along. The automatic settings may handle many decisions for you, like when to use the flash or where to focus, but that won't be the case every time you push the button. For all the technology contained in your camera, there will be times you will need to let the camera know who's in charge. And as with any camera, you have to compose a shot.

The first rule of photographic composition is that there are no hard and fast rules. But there are considerations, not all immediately obvious, that can enhance how a shot will look. As the photographer, you will use your own aesthetic sense to determine the best way to achieve the look you want in each shot.

Setting Up a Shot

When you're ready to take a picture, check first that the obvious things are correct. Make sure that the camera is on and the lens cap is off. Before you push the button, also check that your finger or camera strap is not in front of the lens.

This is also a good time to check the camera settings like flash and file type (which we'll cover in detail in Chapter 4).

One of the secrets to composing a good photo is patience. Before you push the shutter button, take a moment to look closely at the composition. Elements of a photograph include not just your main subject, but also the foreground (the area in front of the subject, or the subject itself if you're shooting close up), the background (the area behind the subject, or in the distance), and the objects to either side. Look through the viewfinder and consider the arrangement of the elements. Do the other elements in the shot draw the eye toward or away from the subject? Are there elements that distract from the subject? Will the shot give the viewer a sense of size or distance, (**Figures 3.1** and **3.2**)? Do the elements in the shot tell the story (**Figure 3.3**)? Will turning the camera vertically include more of what you want in the shot, or eliminate distractions to the side (**Figure 3.4**)?

Figure 3.1 The water in the foreground (made to look deeper and farther away by tilting the camera down), combined with the haze, gives a sense of how long a swim it is from Alcatraz.

Figure 3.2 Tilting the camera up to include more background emphasizes how big the sky really is on the plains of western Nebraska.

Figure 3.3 The sign and the book, as well as the crowd in the background, give a sense of where Adam is and what he's doing there.

Figure 3.4 Here are two different takes on Canyon de Chelly in Arizona. Each gives a different visual sense of Spider Rock.

One of the common mistakes photographers make is not keeping the camera level as they shoot. Make sure that the camera is level (right to left) so that you don't get off-kilter horizontal lines in the shot (**Figure 3.5**).

Figure 3.5 Because the camera was not level, the horizontal line is at an angle in the shot.

Framing the Shot

Before you push the shutter, take a look at what you see through the viewfinder. See if there is anything in the shot that will distract from the subject. Try moving to one side or zooming for a different look.

A classic error in composition is the tree growing out of a subject's head (**Figure 3.6**). Before you push the shutter button, take a moment to study all of the elements in the frame. There may be subtle elements that will distract the eye from the subject or that will look positively silly. By moving the camera or subject slightly, you can eliminate the unwanted effect (**Figure 3.7**).

Figure 3.6 The tree branches look like antlers when Megan stands directly in front of the tree.

Figure 3.7 By moving her to the side, both Megan and the tree can be in the shot, but the antler effect is gone.

Avoiding Framing Problems (Parallax)

In order for you to see what you're taking a picture of, a camera has to have a viewfinder. There are two types of viewfinders: *reflex* (single lens) and *optical* (double lens).

A reflex system, sometimes called *single lens reflex* (SLR), allows you to see what the camera sees. When you look through the lens, the image you see is coming through the same lens that will be used to take the picture. The image is reflected on a mirror up into the viewfinder that you look through. When you take the picture, the mirror flips out of the way momentarily so the image can be seen by the camera sensor (hence the term *reflex*). The downside of this design is that the mechanism that moves the lens is more expensive to manufacture, so reflex systems are used only on the most expensive professional-level cameras.

Most digital cameras use a double-lens system. In addition to the lens that takes the picture, there is a second lens above it that you look through. The problem with a double-lens system is that you are not seeing exactly what the camera sees. This slight offset between the views is called *parallax*. For most shots the difference is so small that it doesn't present a problem. But for close-ups, you could wind up with the classic cut-off head effect (**Figure 3.8**). Some cameras have marks visible through the viewfinder that give you an idea of what will be in the shot.

Figure 3.8 In the viewfinder Juli's head appeared to be in the shot, but it didn't entirely make it into the frame of the actual photo.

Fortunately, digital cameras also have the LCD screen viewer. Since the image that you see on the screen is coming through the main lens, you'll see the shot properly framed. Unfortunately, you can't always use the LCD to frame a shot. For instance, in bright sunlight, you probably won't be able to see the image on the screen; you'll have to rely on the viewfinder instead. In such a case, you should always allow some extra room around the subject to avoid cutting off important bits. You can always crop out the extra room later.

*A screen hood is an inexpensive solution to the problem of not being able to see the LCD in bright light. For about $20, you can get a small hood with a flexible band that holds it on the camera. The hood shields the screen from the light, so you can see what's going on (**Figure 3.9**).*

Figure 3.9 A screen hood will let you see the LCD display even in bright sunlight.

Choosing the Optimum Distance

Since most digital cameras have a zoom feature, you can reframe shots with the push of a button. By zooming in, you

can change the apparent distance between the subject and the camera. But if you're too close to the subject, you might not be able to get the background in focus (if that's what you want). Your best strategy in such a case is to step back from the subject and use the zoom (**Figure 3.10**).

For portraits, a wide-angle lens setting will distort things that are close up, making the subject look a bit chubbier. Moving away from the subject and using the zoom to frame the shot will give you a more flattering picture (**Figure 3.11**).

Figure 3.10 The autofocus chose the bush in the foreground, leaving the background out of focus.

Figure 3.11 This portrait is less than flattering because the zoom was set to wide angle. Moving back and zooming in makes Veronica look much better.

If you're shooting with the flash and you're too close, the flash will often create too harsh a light. As with the wide-angle distortion, this is easily solved by moving further back and zooming in.

If your flash is creating too harsh a light, you can use an old photographer's trick: Hold or tape a bit of tissue paper over the flash on the front of the camera. This will create a softer, more diffused light.

Determining What's in Focus

Most digital cameras have an autofo-cus feature. When you point the cam-era at your subject, the camera will automatically focus on it. The autofo-cus on most cameras uses what's in the center of the viewfinder to determine the proper focus. But you may want to change the focus for a particular shot. For instance, you can often get a bet-ter shot if you leave the background out of focus, which places the empha-sis on the foreground (**Figure 3.12**).

Figure 3.12 The cannon in the foreground stands out in this shot because the background is slightly out of focus.

To overcome the autofocus feature, point the camera at the part of the picture you want in focus and hold the shutter but-ton halfway down. Reframe the shot while continuing to hold down the button, and then push the button all the way down to take the picture. Now the focus will be on the part of the picture you targeted.

Sometimes the autofocus feature is less than accurate. Two com-mon examples are when there's low contrast between the sub-ject and the background and when there are lines in front of the subject (**Figure 3.13**). In these situations, the point-and-hold technique above may (or may not) overcome the problem.

Figure 3.13 Because the cage's vertical lines are closer than the bird, the camera auto-focused on the bars, leaving the bird is slightly out of focus.

Composing According to the Rule of Thirds

Your first instinct when you set up a shot will often be to put the subject in the center of the frame. But that doesn't always make for an interesting photograph.

Photographers use the *Rule of Thirds*, dividing the picture frame into nine sections. Visualize a tic-tac-toe grid of evenly spaced horizontal and vertical lines (**Figure 3.14**). By putting the main subject at (or near) one of the four intersections of these lines, you can create a more interesting shot, as the viewer's eye is naturally drawn to elements at those intersections.

Don't feel that you have to use this rule in every shot. Like most rules, it's there to be broken. But you'll probably find that most photos look better with this kind of balance.

Figure 3.14 With the mesa in the center of this picture, the result is your basic snapshot. By reframing to either side, with the mesa at an intersection of the invisible grid lines, you get a more dramatic shot.

Working with the Light

When shooting a photo in available light (like sunlight), set up the shot so that the light source is behind the camera. If the light is behind the subject, the camera's autoexposure will overcompensate for the bright light, leaving the subject underexposed. You can compensate for the exposure (see "Shooting Against the Light"), but details will still often get lost in the shadows (**Figure 3.15**).

Figure 3.15 The details of the trees are lost because the light is behind them.

If you don't have the option to set up the shot with the light behind the camera, you can try to position the light to one side. Regardless of where the light is coming from, take note of how the shadows are affecting the subject. Often a shot will look good at first glance, but when you view at full size, details will be obscured in shadow. If you're not sure how it's going to look, try shooting the same shot from different angles, taking note of the shadows as you experiment (**Figure 3.16**).

Figure 3.16 Shooting the same tree from different angles produces differing shadow effects.

Gauging the Light Source

It's not always easy (or possible) to tell exactly how the existing light will affect a shot as you take it. Bright sunlight will sometimes wash out details in the brightest area (**Figure 3.17**).

Figure 3.17 The bright sunlight drowns out the details where it shines the brightest.

If you're not sure that the autoexposure setting will give you the shot you want, you can take the shot and then reshoot at different angles and zoom levels. This gives you better odds of having one of the shots come out with an optimal exposure (**Figure 3.18**).

Figure 3.18 At different angles, the highlights and shadows produce contrasting views of Dan's favorite cherry tree.

In Chapter 4, we'll discuss how to use camera features like exposure compensation and fill flash to compensate for tricky lighting situations.

When shooting outdoors, the softer light toward the end of the day will generally give you better looking shots than the bright glare of the midday sun.

Shooting against the Light

If you can't set up a shot so that the light is behind the camera, you can still usually get good results with a little thought and some trial-and-error experimentation.

The autoexposure on most digital cameras uses *center weighting.* This means that the camera determines the best exposure for a shot by sampling the shot in the center of the viewfinder, the same way that autofocus works. When you shoot with the light source behind the subject, you often won't get the right exposure. Because the camera sees so much light, it sets the exposure too low and the darker areas lose detail (**Figure 3.19**).

Figure 3.19 The details in the foreground are lost because of the brightness of the sky in the background.

Fortunately, there's a simple solution: Temporarily reframe the shot so that the subject (the darker area) is in the center of the frame. Press the shutter button halfway down and hold it. (This tells the camera to use that area to set the exposure.) While continuing to hold the button, reframe the shot the way you want it and push the button all the way down to take the picture. Again, this technique is similar to that used to override autofocus (**Figure 3.20**).

Figure 3.20 The bright sky in the background fooled the autoexposure into underexposing, and the faces are too dark. Fixing the autoexposure on the faces makes Kaitlyn and Kayla look much better.

Sometimes there will be too big a difference between the brightest and darkest areas to get the exposure just right. In that case, you can use the bright area as a picture element, creating a nice visual contrast with the rest of the picture (**Figure 3.21**).

Figure 3.21 The far entrance to the tunnel is much brighter than the inside, but it creates a nice contrasting effect.

F-Stop and Shutter Speed

Each shot you take will have differing amounts of light. So any camera needs to be adjusted, manually or automatically, for the amount of light, or else your photo will be too dark or light. As we discussed in Chapter 1, cameras use a combination of *aperture* (aka *f-stop*), the size of the hole that the light is coming through; and *shutter speed*, how long the hole is left open to adjust exposure. Most of the time, you can let the camera's electronics determine the exposure automatically and the picture will come out just fine. But sometimes you'll need to control the exposure manually.

Shutter speed can be used to freeze or blur motion. A high shutter speed, where the shutter is opened for a short amount of time, can freeze motion. This is handy for getting a sharp picture of, say, a batter swinging. A low shutter speed, where the shutter is open for a longer time, blurs motion.

Aperture size affects not only how much light is let in through the lens, but also what is in focus. A smaller f-stop will create a greater depth of field, in which more of the picture is in focus, and a larger f-stop will limit what is in focus (**Figure 3.22**).

Figure 3.22 With a shallow depth of field, the flower and spider are in focus, but the background is not.

Changing the f-stop on a digital camera has a much more limited effect on what's in focus than changing it does on larger-format cameras. Digital cameras (except for the high-end models that use 35mm lenses) have short lenses, so their depth of field is large. As a result, most everything in a shot except for extreme close-ups will be in focus.

Shooting Motion

When a subject is in motion, the camera will blur the shot if the shutter speed is too slow (**Figure 3.23**) Sometimes this makes for an interesting effect, but if you want to see the motion

Figure 3.23 The shutter speed was too slow to freeze the motion, so Megan's kicking foot is a blur.

frozen (without a blur), you have to use a faster shutter speed. If your camera has the option to manually set shutter speed, simply adjust it to a faster setting (from, say, 1/60 to 1/125 of a second). Some cameras have an option to set the ISO or film speed. This setting imitates a film camera using a "faster" film (**Figure 3.24**). If you change the ISO setting from 100 to 400, the camera will use a faster shutter speed and give you the frozen motion you're looking for (**Figure 3.25**).

Figure 3.24 With a higher ISO setting, the camera uses a faster shutter speed.

Figure 3.25 With a higher shutter speed, the kicking foot is clear while in motion.

A Word about Portraits

Shooting pictures of people is one of the most common uses for any camera. But shooting a portrait has its challenges. Most people tense up when they're in front of a camera. The secret to getting a good shot is to overcome that tension. Dan's favorite tactics are humor and ambush.

Let the subject get used to be being on camera by not shooting immediately. Telling them a joke or even making a funny noise will get them to relax momentarily. Take that opportunity to get the shot with the more natural expression (**Figure 3.26**).

Figure 3.26 A quick bon mot from Dan got a more natural smile from Betty and Billy.

You can also try the ambush technique. Frame the subject so that they don't see you. Wait for them to turn and face the camera and get the shot in the second before they are able to react (**Figure 3.27**).

Framing a portrait shot with more than just the face will usually give you a better-balanced picture than a full face would (**Figure 3.28**). A head and shoulders shot is also more flattering.

Many times, as in the old cliché, people really do have a "good side." By having subjects turn their head to the side, but look back at the camera with their eyes, you can catch their best side (**Figure 3.29**).

Figure 3.27 Dale didn't see the camera so he didn't have a chance to tense up.

Figure 3.28 Including the upper body gives some balance to the shot.

Figure 3.29 Sonya's best profile is highlighted by having her head turned slightly.

Set the
Camera Options

Digital cameras include many more options than film cameras do. You can use these features to compensate for tricky lighting or artificial light, to change the framing with the zoom, and to choose the type of file the camera will create for each shot.

In this chapter, we cover the most common features. Obviously, not every camera will have every feature. So your mileage may vary, as the saying goes.

Resolution

On a digital camera, the resolution setting controls both the file type and the size of the photograph that is saved to the storage card. All cameras can save in JPEG format. Some also offer the higher-resolution TIFF and RAW formats. Within each format setting, you can also choose the resolution or number of pixels that the picture will contain. The more pixels, the higher the resolution and the larger you can display or print the picture without compromising quality.

Choosing the Right Resolution for Your Purpose

Before you choose the resolution setting for a photo, consider what you plan to do with the picture. If you plan to print a shot, you'll want the highest quality file format (TIFF or RAW). If you plan to display the picture on a Web page or send it via email, you can use JPEG.

Next, you choose the resolution. Some cameras have several resolution settings with names like SHQ (super high quality), also called Fine; HQ (high quality), or Normal; and SQ (standard quality), or Basic. The resolution setting determines the image size and the amount of information the camera saves for each picture.

You might think that you should simply take all of your pictures at the highest resolution so you'll get the best quality. There are several reasons why this is impractical. First, the higher the resolution, the larger the file size. And the larger the file size, the fewer pictures you'll be able to fit on the storage card. For example, if your camera came with an 8 MB or 16 MB card, you might only be able to save one or two pictures at the highest resolution. Unless you plan to make a major investment in storage media, and few people do, that's a pretty big limitation.

Another reason you won't want to use the highest resolution is the law of diminishing returns. If your plan is to ultimately display the photo on your Web site, the higher resolution is a waste of space, since the extra pixels are going to be thrown away when you reduce the size of the picture. See Chapter 10 for a chart of image sizes and their respective print sizes.

Remember that you can mix file types and sizes on the same card. So you can use different formats for different pictures just by changing the settings.

Setting Resolution on the Camera

Most cameras offer two methods for changing settings. You can set the most commonly used features, like flash settings, via buttons on the camera (**Figure 4.1**). Most of the settings are accessed using a menu. The menu is displayed on the camera's LCD display (**Figure 4.2**). To learn how to specify the settings on your particular camera, refer to the documentation.

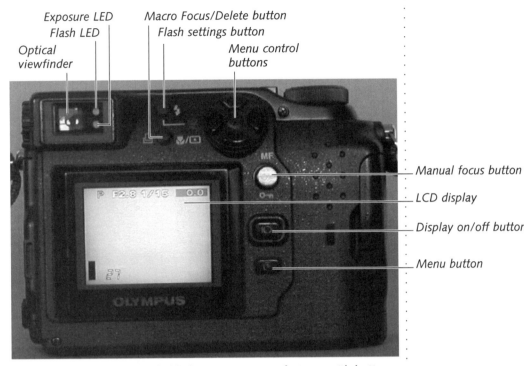

Exposure LED
Flash LED

Macro Focus/Delete button
Flash settings button

Optical
viewfinder

Menu control
buttons

Manual focus button

LCD display

Display on/off button

Menu button

Figure 4.1 Your camera probably lets you set most features with buttons.

Figure 4.2 Menu choices are displayed on the screen.

Some cameras have an option that lets you choose whether to have the camera save your setting changes or return to the defaults when you shut it off. Check your camera's documentation.

Focus

To get your subject in focus, the camera lens must be set to the right distance. Autofocus will give you the right setting in the vast majority of cases.

45

Using Autofocus

For most pictures, you can use the autofocus by pointing the camera at the subject and simply pressing the shutter button. The camera measures the distance to the subject and adjusts the focus accordingly. What could be easier?

Unfortunately, that doesn't always do the job. There are a few situations in which autofocus will not work correctly without a little input from the user. If the subject is not in the center of the frame or there's an excessively bright object near the center (where autofocus will look to determine proper focus), then autofocus may not gauge the distance correctly (**Figure 4.3**).

Figure 4.3 Setting the focus while aiming at the street and then reframing on the car prevents the glare on the windshield from throwing the autofocus off.

If you're not sure that the autofocus is going to know what you're trying to focus on, temporarily move the camera so that the intended subject is in the center of the frame and hold the shutter button halfway down to set the focus, Then reframe the shot, and press the button all the way (**Figure 4.4**).

Figure 4.4 Autofocus focused on the closer car, slightly blurring the background (left). Setting the autofocus using the background keeps it in focus, but slightly blurs the car in the foreground (right).

Using Manual Focus

If your camera offers a manual focus option, you can set the focus yourself. Since the viewfinder will not always reliably show good focus, you should measure the distance from the camera to the subject. Then set the focus on the camera to that distance (**Figure 4.5**).

Figure 4.5 The manual focus display aids you in setting a proper focus distance.

Using Macro Focus

At normal settings, the closest you can get to a subject and still have it in focus is about 10 to 12 inches. When you want a super-close shot of something like a flower, you'll need to set the camera to macro focus. At this setting, you can get within a couple of inches and the autofocus will correctly adjust for that distance (**Figure 4.6**).

Figure 4.6 The camera was about 3 inches from the flower and was set to macro focus.

When reviewing your photos, the LCD display on your camera is too small to give you a reliable sense of whether a shot is in focus. Always check the shot on your computer to make sure that the fine points like focus are correct.

Exposure

Any camera must be set to allow just the right amount of light in order to get a properly exposed picture. Fortunately, digital cameras are very smart and do this automatically. But there are some situations that call for your input to make a photo come out the way that you want it to.

Many cameras give you the ability to set *shutter speed* (the length of the exposure) and *aperture* (how much light is let in for the exposure) manually.

What Does Autoexposure Do?

Autoexposure gauges the proper amount of light required to get a good shot. As with autofocus, autoexposure will do the job in most situations; but there are some situations where it won't properly gauge the correct exposure. Autoexposure, like autofocus, uses the center of the frame to measure the light. So if there is a particularly bright or dark area near the center of the frame, it will throw the exposure off.

To compensate, temporarily move the camera so that the area with the amount of light that you want is in the center of the frame, and hold the shutter button halfway down. Then reframe the shot, and press the button all the way to take the picture (**Figure 4.7**).

Figure 4.7 The sun behind the trees caused the autoexposure to underexpose this shot (left). Aiming the center of the viewfinder at the ground and holding the shutter button halfway down caused the autoexposure to use the darker area to set the exposure (right).

Setting Shutter Priority

Some cameras let you manually set the shutter speed while having the autoexposure set the appropriate aperture automatically. You can use this Shutter Priority option if you're trying to capture a subject in motion and you want to either freeze the motion (with a faster shutter) or blur it (with a slower shutter) (**Figure 4.8**).

Figure 4.8 With a fast shutter speed, the motion of Sarah on the mower is frozen. With a slower shutter speed, the mower looks like it's going at a much faster clip.

Setting Aperture Priority

Aperture Priority works much the same as Shutter Priority, except that you set the f-stop and the camera then chooses the right shutter speed. This can be useful if you want to increase the depth of field. Because aperture on most digital cameras doesn't have as noticeable an effect on depth of field as with a larger camera, this is not a feature you're likely to use much.

Using Manual Exposure

For the adventurous or advanced photographer, some cameras offer a manual exposure option. You can set both the shutter speed and the aperture yourself. You'll have to gauge the proper exposure on your own. You can try taking several shots at different settings and reviewing each shot on the camera's display to figure out the optimum setting (**Figure 4.9**).

Figures 4.9 Three different manual exposures on the same subject show more and less light. Shoot it several different ways, and you can then choose the one that work best.

Setting Exposure Compensation

If you want to use the autoexposure but still want a degree of control, some cameras offer *exposure compensation*. With this feature, you can set the autoexposure to be slightly lighter or darker to tone down glare in very bright sunlight or to enhance highlights in deep shade.

Most exposure compensation controls measure the compensation as positive and negative decimal numbers. Setting a positive number will make the picture brighter and a negative number will make it darker (**Figure 4.10**).

Figure 4.10 The first shot of Dan's lawn tractor was set with a positive exposure compensation setting, creating a brighter shot. The middle shot was set with no exposure compensation. The last shot was taken with a negative exposure compensation setting, resulting in a darker image.

Setting White Balance

If you're shooting in certain kinds of lighting, such as indoors with artificial light, you can wind up with odd-looking results. Because artificial light has different amounts of color than natural light, a shot may wind up looking too red or too green. (See "Correcting Color Shifts" in Chapter 9.) Digital cameras have a marvelous feature called *white balance* that will correct this kind of problem before it happens. By setting the camera to automatically correct for different types of light as you shoot, you can get a good-looking photograph without having to do extensive color correction in your image-editing software.

White balance can be set to correct for:

- Incandescent light
- Fluorescent light

- Cloudy outdoor light
- Bright outdoor light (full sunshine)

Most cameras also have an automatic setting that will determine the best white balance setting (**Figure 4.11**). But there are no set rules about white balance. Every camera handles it a bit differently, so a bit of experimentation will give you a sense of what works best.

If you're using a flash to shoot, you may not have to worry about color correction—the flash will provide properly balanced light. But if the flash will only cover the subject, the background may still show a color imbalance. So in that case you'd use the white balance.

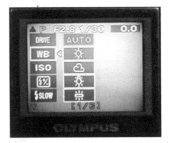

Figure 4.11 The default white balance setting on most cameras is Auto.

Zoom

The ability to zoom is one of the handiest features on a camera. Rather than having to move yourself closer or farther from a subject, you can use the zoom to change the apparent distance. So you can make your subject appear to be closer to the camera by zooming in, or you can widen the field to get more in a shot by zooming out (**Figure 4.12**).

Figure 4.12 Three different views of the same scene, taken in the same spot, using the zoom to change the framing.

Digital cameras (depending on your model) use optical and/or digital zoom. Optical zoom uses the lens to magnify the subject and will give you a good photo at full resolution. Digital zoom can get you closer to the subject, but it enlarges the image using the circuitry in the camera, much the way you'd enlarge it using image editing software—and with the same effect. Digital zoom results in a lower-quality picture (**Figure 4.13**).

The bottom line is that you should stick with optical zoom unless it's absolutely necessary to get a closer shot.

Figure 4.13 Even though the second, digitally zoomed, shot brings Megan and her friends in closer, it loses detail and sharpness that is there in the first shot.

Using Optical Zoom

The zoom control allows you to reframe a shot without moving. This is incredibly convenient and is thus a feature that you'll use a lot. You can change from a wide angle to a close-up without moving an inch. Typically, you'll find the zoom control on the top of the camera. Just look through the viewfinder (or LCD display), and push the zoom button to move in or out.

Using Digital Zoom

Most digital cameras with both optical and digital zoom are set to use the optical zoom by default. If you find that you want to get a closer shot, you can change the setting to keep going beyond the optical zoom's range. As you zoom, the display will indicate where optical zoom stops and digital zoom begins (**Figure 4.14**).

Figure 4.14 The zoom indicator shows you when you've gone past optical zoom territory and into digital zoom.

Flash

When there isn't enough available light to take a good picture, the camera needs help, in the form of a flash. The flash adds enough light to give the proper exposure.

Most cameras will automatically use the flash when they detect that more light is required. Most cameras have an indicator light that lets you know that the flash is ready. After you use the flash on a shot, there will usually be a few seconds' delay while the flash recharges (**Figure 4.15**).

Figure 4.15 The upper LED flashes when the flash is not ready to fire or if there isn't enough light (if the flash is turned off).

When using the flash, keep in mind that most flashes don't throw their light more than 10 or 15 feet. Anything beyond that range will not get enough light for a proper exposure.

Some cameras have an external flash option. This is a jack where you can plug in a separate, more powerful flash unit.

Reducing Red Eye

One of the problems that arise when you're shooting a portrait shot with flash is the dreaded "red-eye" effect. When the flash goes off, the human eye's iris reflects the flash as a bright red. Since you generally don't want a subject to look like a movie monster, this is not good. Most cameras offer a red-eye reduction flash setting. This setting will fire the flash twice, once to let the subject's eye adjust to the light (which eliminates the red eye) and then again a second later when the picture is actually taken. Make sure when using the red-eye setting that your subject knows that the flash will fire twice, so they don't move between flashes.

Red eye can be corrected on your computer with image-editing software, but it's preferable to eliminate it at the source.

Using the Flash to Fill In Light

When shooting a subject in shadows, you might sometimes want just a bit of flash to bring out the darker areas without making everything too bright. *Fill flash* is the answer. When set to fill flash, the camera uses a reduced amount of flash, which is usually just enough to bring out the details in the darker areas (**Figure 4.16**).

Figure 4.16 With no flash, the darker areas like the hair lack detail. By adding some fill flash, there's enough light to see the shadow details without washing out the brighter areas.

Shooting without the Flash

Most cameras give you the option to suppress the flash. If there isn't sufficient light to get a good exposure but you don't want to use a flash, you can turn it off entirely. The camera will adjust the exposure setting accordingly. This setting can come in handy in, say, a museum that doesn't allow flash photography. It will also be useful if the subject is behind or near a shiny surface that will reflect too much light in the shot (**Figure 4.17**).

But there's a catch. (Isn't there always?) In low light and with no flash, the shutter speed may be so slow that the shot will come out blurred. As a rule, any shutter speed slower than 1/30th of a second will be blurred if you're holding the camera. As long as your subject doesn't move, you can overcome this problem by using a tripod or monopod. This will generally keep the camera steady enough get a clear shot even at low shutter speed (**Figure 4.18**).

Figure 4.17 The glare of the flash on the glass from washes out this shot of a poster.

Figure 4.18 Turning the flash off and using a monopod to hold the camera steady results in a good, sharp shot.

Shooting at Night

When you're shooting outdoors at night, the flash will illuminate the subject, but the shutter speed may be too fast to capture anything not in the flash's range. If you want to capture a portion of the background, some cameras offer a night flash, or slow shutter, setting. With this setting, the flash will fire, but the shutter will stay open longer to capture the darker areas of the shot (**Figure 4.19**).

Figure 4.19 With the standard flash setting, the tree and house are illuminated by the flash (left). The night flash setting still illuminates the house and tree, but you can also see the light through the window (right).

Flash Correction

If you want to use the flash but find that it's too light or dark or just too glaring, some cameras offer a flash correction option. As with exposure compensation, you can set the flash to be brighter or darker. This can be helpful if you find that the flash is washing out highlight details (**Figure 4.20**).

Figure 4.20 Two different flash correction settings show the same banjo with more and less glare.

*If you need the flash to get a shot but find that the flash is creating too much reflection when you're pointing the camera directly at the subject, try shooting at an angle to eliminate the glare (**Figure 4.21**).*

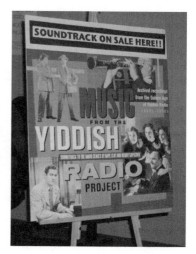

Figure 4.21 The glossy surface of the poster reflects too much flash and creates a glare. By shooting at an angle, you eliminate the reflection, but the poster is still readable.

Self-Timer/Remote Control

If you'd like to take a picture and be in it at the same time, you can use the self-timer function. Set up the shot, and turn on the self-timer. The camera will wait 10 to 20 seconds after you push the shutter button before actually taking the picture, giving you time to run and get in the shot.

In case it needs to be said, the self-timer/remote control requires that the camera be on a tripod or other stationary object.

Some cameras offer a remote control, which allows you to simply press the button on a little remote gizmo to take the picture (**Figure 4.22**).

The self-timer/remote can also be useful if you're taking a tripod shot and don't want to shake the camera when pushing the shutter button.

Figure 4.22 Kaity became a photographer by pushing the button on the remote control and taking her own picture.

Store and Transfer Your Photos

Once you've taken your photographs, you'll want to be able to look at them...again and again, in fact. You can do so immediately by reviewing them right on the camera. But the camera storage card is not a good place to keep them, at least not for long. You'll want to move them to your computer, where they're safer and more useful. Once there, you can see them with more detail, save them in a variety of formats, and make backup copies.

This chapter gets your pictures out of the camera, into your computer, and organized for future use.

Choose Your Images

Using the camera's LCD display, you can look at your photographs right after you take them. Because the screen is so small, you'll only be able to get a general sense of what a shot looks like. But that will be enough to determine whether the shot came out, the exposure was good, and the shot was framed properly. The finer points, like sharp focus, will be better viewed when you transfer the shots to your computer.

Viewing Stored Images

To view the shots stored on your camera, set the camera to *viewing mode* (also called *Playback mode*). The shots will appear on the camera's display (**Figure 5.1**). Use the buttons on the camera to move from one shot to the next. If you've had a busy day of shooting, you can swap cards to view all of your shots. If your camera has the option to zoom in on each shot, you can get a better view of the finer aspects, like focus.

Figure 5.1 When in Playback mode, the camera becomes the viewer that enables you to see the shots inside.

Most cameras offer a feature that allows you to lock your favorite shots to prevent accidental deletion. Typically, this button looks like a key (**Figure 5.2**). While a shot is on the display, press the lock key and you won't be able to delete the shot until you unlock it.

Figure 5.2 When you're viewing photos, the OK button (with the image of a key underneath) will lock a shot to prevent deletion.

Some cameras have functions that let you edit shots while you're reviewing them. You can change a shot to black and white or sepia tone, for example, or add filter effects like starbursts in the bright highlights. We strongly recommend against using these features. You can do the same kind of processing more effectively later with image-editing software without changing the original shot.

Deleting an Unwanted Shot

As you review your photos, you'll probably find shots that you don't want to keep. You can delete these shots on the camera, freeing up room on the storage card. As you view the unwanted shot, press the Delete button on the camera (**Figure 5.3**). (This button often has an icon like a wastebasket.) The camera will ask if you really want to delete the shot. Press OK to confirm and the shot will be gone.

Figure 5.3 The Flash settings button serves as the Delete button in Playback mode.

As on a computer, once you've deleted a file, it's really gone. So if you are not sure, err on the side of caution and keep the shot until you can review it on your computer. You can always delete it later.

Conserving Battery Life

The single biggest drain on battery life with digital cameras is the display. The longer you leave the display on, the faster your batteries will fail. So minimize your use of the display whenever possible. Only review your shots on the camera when you need to free up space on the storage card. Or carry *lots* of batteries.

If your camera offers the option to run with an AC adapter, you can use that to preserve battery life whenever you're near an outlet.

Connect to Your Computer

The best method for connecting your digital camera to your computer is with a Universal Serial Bus (USB) port. USB connections are fast and easily configured. Not all cameras offer a USB connection, however. Some require a serial port. Serial ports have a slower data transfer rate than USB ones. If a serial connection is your only option, seriously consider getting a card reader. Card readers will give you a much faster transfer rate than a camera-to-serial port connection. (We cover card readers in Chapter 2.)

If your computer doesn't have a USB port, you can generally add one using a USB PCI card (for desktop computers) or PC Card (for laptops). These cards are generally inexpensive (under $40) and fairly easy to install.

To connect your camera to your computer, check the camera's documentation to see if you must install software first. If so, follow the instructions provided.

If you're connecting the camera via a USB port, you can usually just plug the camera in, even with the computer running. If you're connecting with a serial port, check your manual to see if you need to shut the computer off before connecting the camera (you usually do).

Connecting Directly to Your Computer

When you connect your camera directly to a Windows computer (as opposed to using a card reader), you'll need to run

Figure 5.4 The Sony reader for Windows uses PictureGear Lite to transfer the files; which the software immediately opens as thumbnails for viewing.

the software that came with the camera to view and transfer shots (**Figure 5.4**). After you plug in the camera, either to a serial or USB port, start up the software and follow the instructions.

With a Macintosh (assuming your operating system is version 8.5 or higher), a USB-equipped camera that you plug into your Mac will appear on your desktop as an icon that looks like a disk drive. Double-click the icon to open it, then copy your shots by dragging them to a folder on your hard drive.

Connecting a Card Reader to Your Computer

Card readers are especially useful on a Windows computer. Unlike with direct camera connections, the card reader shows up like a disk drive, so you don't need any software (other than the USB support drivers) to transfer photos.

Before you connect your card reader, check the documentation to see how to install the drivers. Follow those instructions, plug in the reader, and restart the computer. Insert a storage card into the reader. Double-click the My Computer icon, and you'll see the reader listed as a drive (**Figure 5.5**).

When using a Mac, you can just plug the card reader into a USB port (or hub). Insert a storage card in the reader, and it will appear on the desktop (**Figure 5.6**).

Important: Always make sure that the camera is turned off before you remove the storage card.

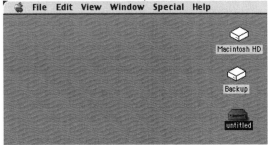

Figure 5.6 The drive icon called Untitled is the card in the reader.

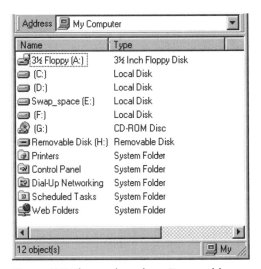

Figure 5.5 The card reader—Removable Disk H:—is displayed in My Computer as it were another disk drive.

When purchasing a card reader, make sure you get a model that's compatible with your storage cards. It's easy to get confused between similarly named formats like Compact Flash Type I and Type II, which are similar but not the same physical size. Without an adapter, you can't use a Type I card in a Type II slot.

Organize Your Computer for Images

Before transferring files to your computer, you should create a destination folder to store them. On a Macintosh, choose File > New Folder. This will create an icon called "untitled folder" (**Figure 5.7**). Click on the folder name and rename it appropriately. In Windows, right-click and choose New > Folder. Right-click on the new folder and choose Rename. Give the new folder a more descriptive name (**Figure 5.8**).

Figure 5.7 A new folder on a Mac is called "untitled folder."

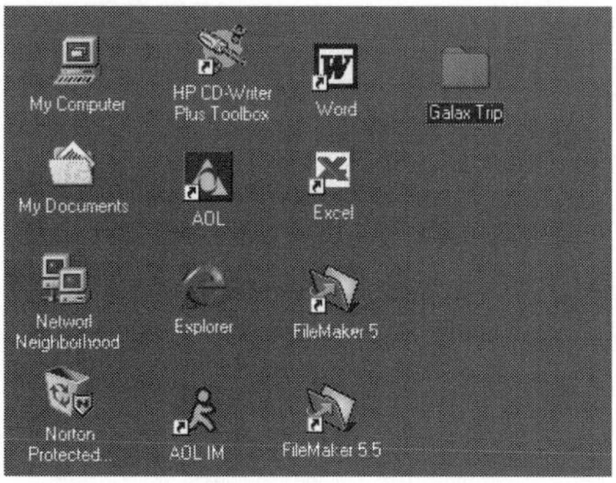

Figure 5.8 Assigning a more descriptive name than New Folder will help organize your shots.

Another important step is to check that your computer has enough available hard drive space. A single digital photograph can take up more than 500 kilobytes (KB) (half a megabyte). Multiply this by the different versions you'll save of the same photo, and your pictures will gobble up space fast. As we discussed earlier, if your hard drive space is running low, you may have to either make more room (by deleting files) or add a second drive.

Transfer Your Photos

Before doing anything with your digital photographs, you must transfer them to your computer. This is *very* important. Never make any changes to your shots while they're still on the storage card.

Some storage cards are locked when you use them on your computer, so you can copy *from* them but not *to* them. If your card is not locked, it's easy to get excited about seeing a picture right away and forget to copy it from the card before tinkering with it. In a word, *don't*. It's very important that you work on a copy of the picture, not the original, so you always have a copy intact.

There's another good reason not to tamper with your original photos on your card. Storage cards are set up with a universal format that's readable by any computer. If you save any changes to the card while it's in the computer, it can corrupt that format and you'll have to reformat the card in the camera—which will wipe out any pictures still on the card.

Transferring Photos from Flash Card to Computer

With your storage card inserted in the reader, the card will be listed as a drive and you can use it just like a drive. Double-click the card reader's drive icon to open it. Most cameras store the photos in a folder (which may actually be inside another folder) on the card. Open the folders on the card until you see the photo files with suffixes like .jpg or .tif (**Figure 5.9**). Those are the files you want to copy to your hard drive.

The easiest way to transfer the files to your hard drive is to choose Select All in the Edit menu and then use the mouse to drag the selected files to a folder on your hard drive (**Figure 5.10**).

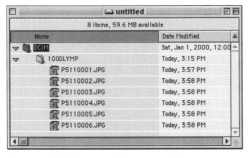

Figure 5.9 The card from an Olympus camera stores the shots in the Olympus folder, which is in the DCIM folder.

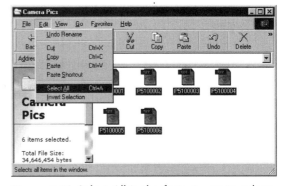

Figure 5.10 Select All is the fastest way to select every file in a folder.

If you use an editing program with an Acquire feature (such as iPhoto or Photoshop Elements), you can use it to copy the files from the card onto your hard drive.

*Windows users: If it's more convenient, after you select the files on the card you can right-click on any of the files and choose Copy. (**Figure 5.11**). Then navigate to the folder on your hard drive, right-click again, and choose Paste.*

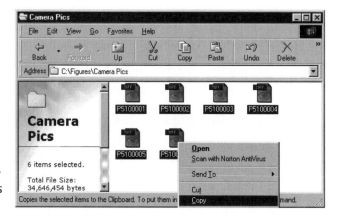

Figure 5.11 In Windows, right-clicking on a file and selecting Copy is an alternative way to transfer files from one folder to another.

Transferring Photos with Infrared Connection

If both your computer and your camera offer infrared connection, you may be able to transfer your photos with no physical connection between the two devices. Check your camera's documentation for instructions on installing the necessary software. Aim the infrared ports on the computer and camera at each other and follow the instructions to transfer the photos.

Take note that in our experience, infrared connections are both slow and unreliable. You will undoubtedly be happier using a direct connection or a card reader.

Erasing Your Flash Card

Once you've transferred your shots from the card (and double-checked to make sure they copied OK), you can erase them from the card so it's ready for action again.

On a Macintosh, select the files, drag them to the Trash and choose Special > Empty Trash. The files are gone and your card is back to maximum capacity.

In Windows, select the files, right-click, and choose Delete (**Figure 5.12**).

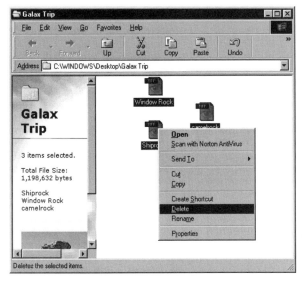

Figure 5.12 You can drag files to the trash in Windows, but right-clicking on selected files and then choosing Delete is a convenient alternative.

Never delete the folders that appear on the card—just the photo files. If the folders get deleted, you'll have to reformat the card in the camera.

If you use an editing program that has an Acquire feature, check the instructions to see what the software does to the files on the card after they're transferred. iPhoto, for instance, will by default automatically erase the card after the files are transferred. You can set the preferences not to do this.

Swapping Flash Cards

After you've transferred your photos from the storage card, you'll want to eject the card from the reader (or from the camera if you're connected directly). On a Windows computer, you can just eject the card.

On a Macintosh, there's an important extra step. You must first either drag the card's drive icon to the Trash or click on it and choose File > Put Away (**Figure 5.13**). If you eject the card without doing one of those two things, you'll make your computer cranky and you may have to restart it.

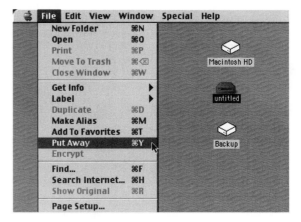

Figure 5.13
Make sure to Put Away a storage card (or drag it to the Trash) before ejecting it.

If Macintosh File Sharing is turned on when you're using a card reader, you may have trouble ejecting the card. To be safe, go to the File Sharing control panel and click Stop to turn the feature off before inserting the card.

View Your Transferred Photos

Once you've transferred your photos to the computer, you'll want to review them to see which to keep, which to send to friends, and of course which duds to dump. Your image-editing software will provide a convenient way to see all of the shots in a particular folder. They'll appear as small "thumbnail" images. You can then double-click on any thumbnail to see the shot full size.

Viewing Your Photos on a Computer

To see photos that you've transferred to your computer, start your image-editing software. (For this example, we'll use Adobe Photoshop Elements.)

Click the File Browser tab, then click the folder list at the top of the window (**Figure 5.14**). Choose the folder you want to browse. The File Browser window will display all of the files in the chosen folder (**Figure 5.15**).

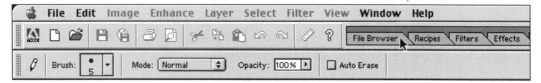

Figure 5.14 Click Elements' File Browser tab to choose a folder to browse.

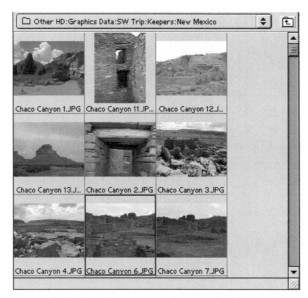

Figure 5.15 The File Browser shows all of the pictures in a folder.

To open a photo, double-click on the thumbnail. With the file open, you can make changes to it or save it with a different name. You can skip the browsing part and just open each file directly in your editing software, but you'll probably save yourself from opening a lot of wrong files if you use the thumbnails.

Viewing Your Photos on a TV

Some cameras can plug in to a television for you to view pictures.

Plug one end of the video cable into the TV's video input jack (usually the yellow one) and the other end into the video output jack on the camera. Set the TV input to Video (or Line In). Switch the camera to Playback mode. Your pictures will appear on the TV screen (**Figure 5.16**).

It may be more convenient to plug the camera into your VCR, since most VCRs have a video input jack on the front (**Figure 5.17**). Set the VCR input to Video (or Line In) and set the TV to view the VCR's output.

Figure 5.16 A television can serve as a big version of the camera's display.

Figure 5.17 Most VCRs have a video input on the front panel.

Save and Organize Photos

The more you use your camera, the more shots you're going to have to keep track of. It's important to set up a system for organizing your work. You can use the same techniques to organize digital photos as you do to organize any other kind of computer data.

Renaming Transferred Photos

When the camera takes a shot, it gives it a cryptic name like P10001.jpg. This doesn't tell you much about what's in the shot. So it's best to rename images as soon as you transfer them to the computer.

Since you will probably want to see the photo to decide on a name, the easiest method for renaming is to use your image editor to open each shot, then choose File > Save As to give it a new name.

Even if your shots are in JPEG format, you should save them as TIFF files to retain the highest resolution (**Figure 5.18**). (See Chapter 7 for more on file formats.)

When you've finished renaming all the shots in a folder, you can get rid of the ones with the cryptic names.

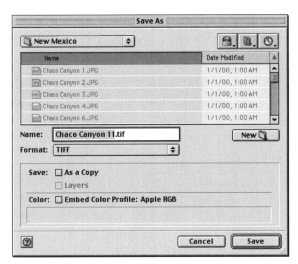

Figure 5.18 Saving files in TIFF format prevents the loss of resolution the JPEG format causes.

Saving Your Originals

As you'll see in the following chapters, you can use the same shot in different ways depending on what you want to do with it. You might have a medium-quality version to post on your Web page and a lower-quality (and therefore smaller) version that you send via email. It's best to save each version with a different name and keep the original unchanged. That way, if later you find another use for it, like making a print, you can use the original at the highest resolution.

Keeping originals also provides you with a safety net if you make changes to a shot in your editing software and those changes aren't exactly what you were looking for.

Organizing Your Photos

Start by creating a folder and calling it something like "Photos." Open that folder and create another folder inside it to store your photographs. You can create as many folders—and as many levels of folders—as you need to logically organize your photos. Then copy each shot to the appropriate folder.

So if you were on vacation in the desert, you might make a folder in your Photos folder for that trip. Inside that folder you might create subfolders for each place you visited and copy the pictures of each place to the appropriate subfolder (**Figure 5.19**). If you kept a journal of your trip, you might organize the folders by date to correspond to your notes.

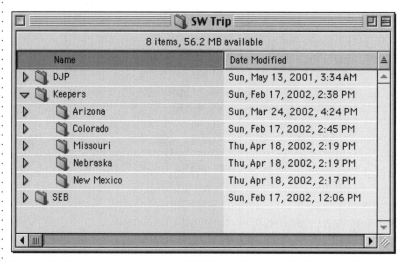

Figure 5.19 A logical structure of folders will make finding a particular photo a lot easier.

Down the line, you'll appreciate the time you took to set up an organizing scheme. A year after your desert trip, you might be hard-pressed to remember details about the shots. But if they're organized properly, you won't have to rely on your memory.

When renaming files, consider using names that describe the specific contents rather than just a date or general area. This will be useful in the future, when the date might not ring a bell, but the name of the shot's subject will.

Burning a CD of Your Images

One of the best ways to preserve your original shots is to burn them (copy them) onto a compact disc (CD). Making a CD allows you to store your photos in their original forms without using hard drive space. If you want to work with a shot in the future, you can just pop in the CD, copy the shot to your hard drive, and do whatever you want to it. A standard CD (also called a CD-R, for recordable) lets you read but not change (rewrite) the data. The advantage of this format is that you'll never have to worry about saving a shot over the original.

Before you create a CD, give some thought to how you'll use it. If you're just going to keep it for your own purposes, format isn't a big deal. But if you intend to send it to others, you might find yourself sending it to someone who works on a different platform than you do. In that case, the format you choose matters.

Most CD-creation software offers you the option to create a *hybrid disc*, which is a universal format that can be read by any computer. If you're creating CDs to share with others, this format is your best bet. If you're not sure what kind of computer will be used to read the CD, opt for this universal format and use filenames no longer than eight characters plus the suffix: GCANYON1.JPG, for example.

A standard CD-R can only be written to once. If you want to reuse CDs, you can try a CD-RW (read/write), which you can erase and use again. But keep in mind that a CD-RW is not readable in all CD players. When sending CDs to others, use a standard CD-R.

You can organize the folders on the CD the same way you do those on your hard drive. Use folders to store the photos by date, place, project—or whatever makes sense for the situation.

To create a CD, start up your CD-creation software, drag the folders containing your photos into the program, and burn away (**Figure 5.20**).

Figure 5.20 A CD will hold up to 675 MB of your photographs— that's a lot of pictures.

Recording Your Images on a VCR

If your camera has a Video Out jack, you can make videotapes of your photos. This is a great way to send a series of photos to someone who doesn't have a computer.

Plug your camera into the Video In jack on the VCR. Insert a blank videotape. Set the VCR to Record. Let it run for a few seconds to get past the *leader* (the nonrecording part of the tape) and then hit Pause. Using the camera's controls, view the first picture you want to record. Start the tape rolling for as long as you want the picture to appear on the tape. Hit Pause, switch to the next picture, and start recording again. Repeat this process for as many pictures as you want to include on the tape.

Organize with iPhoto

As anyone with piles of envelopes full of film prints knows, if you can't find a picture, you might as well not have shot it.

Image-cataloging programs help us to be better at managing digital prints than we usually are with traditional ones.

Although hardly unique, iPhoto exemplifies the types of functions you'd want in image cataloging software. (See "What Makes Good Cataloging Software?" below.) You import your photo files into the program either directly from your camera via a USB cable or from anywhere on your hard disk. Then you have a seemingly infinite number of ways to organize them.

Like all cataloging applications, iPhoto lets you create albums. When you move a photo into an album, it's like creating an alias or shortcut to the real photo in the library. If you delete a photo from an album, the original still remains in the catalog. Unlike with real-world albums, one picture can be placed in multiple albums. So if you have an album of cat pictures, and another album of portraits, that shot of your favorite cat's whiskers could stare out at you from both image collections.

What Makes Good Cataloging Software?

You could think of online photo services as image catalogers, because you can place uploaded photos into albums. (See Chapter 11 for more on online photo services.) But you have very little control over images online. Browser and bandwidth issues make it impossible to change the way images are displayed as you work with them or to see several pictures at once. And what happens when you want to add to the catalog but your allotted space is full? So, if you crave organization, you'll want a program on your own computer.

You'll find lots of options vying for your attention. We think these are nonnegotiable features for cataloging software:

- There should be a variety of ways to import photos—directly from a camera or from anywhere on any disk.

- It should be easy to create and edit captions and labels.

- There should be no limits on how you can organize your photos—by date, occasion, theme, and more.

- You should be able to search by any category, keyword, or text that you used to organize your photos.

- It should be easy to batch groups of photos for labeling, sharing, or exporting—to a Web site, to someplace else on a disk, or even to another cataloging program.

Whether you move a picture into an album or not, you can still catalog it for future organizing. iPhoto automatically labels photos by film roll, which is defined by when you uploaded the photo. You can create keywords for up to 14 categories, then assign one or many keywords to a photo. You can also give each picture its own title and add comments. You can use any text you've typed in the comments section to search for photos; you can also search by film roll, keyword, or title.

Other programs give you similar control over image cataloging. In Windows, Jasc After Shot (www.jasc.com/) and ACDSee (www.acdsystems.com) import images from digital cameras and let you organize them into albums and search on a variety of keywords (**Figure 5.21**). And iView MediaPro for Classic and OS X Mac (a pumped-up, professional organizer for all types of media, not just photos) would keep even a librarian satisfied.

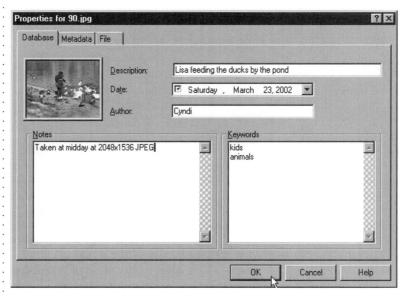

Figure 5.21 ACDSee has a friendly, comprehensive cataloging function.

Choosing Editing Software

6

Using a digital camera opens up your options, whether you're an experienced photographer or a point-and-click snapshot artist. But the camera is only part of what makes the digital experience so satisfying. It's when you combine your camera with your computer that the magic really happens.

There is no single best software choice for picture editing, because everyone has a different definition of what makes a good photo-editing program. What's most important is to realistically match the software to what you want to accomplish, what your computer can handle, and your own skills and talents. There is enough variety in price and features that you should be able to find software that suits your situation, no matter what your level of experience with computers or photography.

Why Do You Need Software?

How perfect are you? Digital cameras make it easier to be a good photographer, because you can immediately see when a photo is really bad. But perfection is as elusive as ever, and never more so than when you're faced with a one-time photo opportunity. When the condor soars over your head in the

Grand Canyon, you can't ask it to do a second flyby because you forgot to change your settings.

Only professional photographers can produce perfectly controlled situations for picture taking, and they use specialized add-ons, lighting, and models to do it. Most great pictures taken under other conditions have a heavy dose of luck involved. Anyone willing to count on pure luck probably doesn't want a digital camera in the first place. So why stop halfway, when you can use software to fix a photo that was shot in the wrong light, crop out that camera strap in the corner, and eliminate Betty's biker boyfriend from the wedding candids after she finally dumped him?

The real question isn't whether you need software. You do, as you'll realize the first time you take a meaningful but flawed picture. The question is what kind of software do you need?

Choosing Software

In some software categories, you-get-what-you-pay-for is the rule. Not necessarily so for photo-editing software. In fact, to do simple edits or repairs of the most common photo errors, many cheapo programs will do the job as well as or better than the name brands.

Even better, you may have exactly what you need on the CD that came with your camera to begin photo editing—emphasis on the word *begin*. Some software that comes with cameras is a stripped-down version of a bigger and better program. You can't even buy it separately, and you can't upgrade it (at least not inexpensively). For example, some cameras still come with Photoshop LE, the light version of Photoshop that Adobe gave away with hardware. When a new version of Photoshop came out you could upgrade your LE program, but only by buying the big Photoshop package. The software company that offers a stripped-down product for free assumes that you'll grow to like the way the software looks and feels so much that you'll buy its big brother when you become more accomplished.

Another type of bundled software you'll find is the consumer photo editor (more on that below). It has lots of recipes and samples for projects users most typically want to create, like calendars or postcards. We think these are a terrific value, and an excellent place to start. They do limit you, though. Because all repairs or projects are push-button, there's not much opportunity for creativity or more professional editing. If you want to cut a photo into an unusual shape or dimension, replace a background, or select a section of a picture to change without changing the rest of the picture, you may not find the tools or recipe you need.

But the nice thing about getting software free with your camera is that you don't have to feel locked into it. If you develop greater ambitions, you can get everything you need from even the biggest names in the business for under $100. Only if you have professional—or professional consumer—interests will your wallet feel the pinch.

Freeware and Shareware vs. Commercial Software

Before launching into a software overview, you should understand the relative merits of freeware, shareware, and commercial software. Although some big players and photo services give away "digital photo" software, most of their free stuff just offers automated functions we call "drop and crop" (see below). If you want software that lets you make *significant* image adjustments without having to pay for it, you'll need to experiment.

We suggest several free packages (called *freeware*) below. Programmers who create these packages won't charge you by the call or the hour if you have a technical problem. In fact, most welcome email and feedback. Many free packages have an enhanced *shareware* version that devotees are more than willing to pay a modest price for after discovering how useful the free version is.

But freeware isn't for everyone. It can make reasonable people with crowded hard drives nervous. Many a Windows computer has been brought low by "something neat I found online." So we've also looked for inexpensive but dependable options from established suppliers. Needless to say, we expect commercial software to meet a higher benchmark of compatibility and longevity than free- or shareware. Companies like Adobe or Microsoft keep their software current with new operating systems. They test their software in different configurations, and if it has conflicts with another major commercial release, they usually find and fix the problem that caused the conflict instead of just ignoring it. Most such companies offer speedy bug fixes for anything really nasty, and you won't have to worry that they won't be in business next year.

Types of Editing Software

Image-editing software falls into several distinct categories, and cost is only part of the picture.

At the low end are free, minimum-function, drop-and-crop programs connected to a photo-printing service. In the middle range are two types of software that have overlapping functions and are frequently confused with each other: image editors and photo editors. And at the high end are professional-level image and photo editors. Image editors are really paint and art programs that let you use photographic images as a starting point. Photo editors share many of the same tools—like brushes or sliders to change brightness and contrast—but arrange them differently. Photo editors frequently have one-button shortcuts for fixing common picture problems, while image editors give you the tools to make these changes but not the recipes for making them.

To confuse the issue even further, many programs with the word *image* or *photo* in their names actually have very limited options for standard photographic manipulation. They have a gazillion flashy ways to turn your photo into a watercolor or a psychedelic flashback, but they may not have an easy way to fix the picture you took indoors where all your friends look pink. Or they are optimized to create photos for the Web, but can't handle the high-resolution images needed for a good photo print.

Software that was designed solely for photo editing will have more tools that affect the entire image rather than part of an image. The tools will emphasize cropping and resizing as well as brightness and contrast fixes rather than painting tools. And any program designed to edit photos will have a red-eye-reduction option; fewer image-editing programs do. If you take lots of close-ups of people indoors, you'll need a program that offers an easy red-eye fix.

Image editors are more likely to provide filters for special effects, masking tools to protect areas of an image from change, and selection tools to let you define these specific areas. If you envision yourself editing out pieces of a picture, or combining pictures with different backgrounds, you'll need these tools (**Figure 6.1**).

Figure 6.1 Image editors like Jasc® Paint Shop Pro (left) and Adobe Photoshop® (above) come with tools that include color pickers and painting tools. Photo editors are more likely to have toolbars that look like this one from Jasc After Shot™ (below). It offers no painting tools, but gives you tools for organizing images into albums and a one-button image repair.

Think long and hard about how much power you really need, especially if you have an older computer or a minimum of RAM (see "Computer Memory and Your Software"). If your computer is more than three years old and you don't want to spend money on upgrading, rethink what you need to do and the tools you need to do it, and lower your expectations. Maybe you should work with an online photo service rather

Computer Memory and Your Software

Ah, but a man's reach should exceed his grasp, Or what's a heaven for? –Robert Browning

Alas, Robert Browning would have seen a lot of frozen cursors on his computer.

People are frequently stunned by how slow—and sometimes unstable—their computers seem when they begin to edit photographs. When they surf the Web, send email, and maybe use a word processor, their computer is more than up to the task. It's only when they open up three high-resolution photos and try to fix their color and run a little filter that it's obvious how much processing power pictures demand. If you try to make a change that takes up more memory than is available, you might wait a long time before anything happens. If your application is not well behaved, you might get a dialog box telling you that it encountered an error and can't save the file. If it's really badly behaved, your application may quit and take your computer down with it.

Such behavior is particularly surprising to people who followed the application's guidance on minimum system configuration; for example:

- 64 MB of RAM
- 150 MB of available hard disk space

Minimums are a little deceptive. This is not the minimum configuration you need to work successfully. It is the minimum configuration the application needs to work at all. The rule of thumb is to take whatever the minimum says and double it. If your computer can't supply the doubled minimum, you should either reconsider buying the program or upgrade your system RAM. Because both Macs and PCs can use hard disk space as virtual memory (storage space temporarily used to run applications), increasing the size of your hard drive can help, too. But we don't recommend virtual memory as a substitute for the real thing. It will sometimes get you out of an immediate jam, but some programs become unstable when they use it. And it's *slow* compared with real RAM.

As long as your computer is not tremendously underpowered, you can maximize its resources by being smart about memory use. Here are some easy short-term fixes for a memory problem:

- Close extra files when you no longer need them. Even if you aren't doing anything to a file, the computer is spending memory just keeping it open.

- Don't open other applications at the same time. Every open application is a memory drain.

- Manage layers. If you are using an editing application that has layers, like Photoshop® Elements or the GIMP, delete layers that don't have anything on them and merge any layers that you can. To see how much space a layer takes up in your application, look at your program's Info box and watch how the file size changes when you add one. That's memory you could use for your real project.

- Save and close a file, then open it again. Many applications remember all the changes you've made to a picture so you can undo them if necessary—lots of changes mean lots of memory is being used. Closing a file clears the history of undos the computer has been holding in memory.

Photoshop for Windows and Photoshop Elements let you change the percentage of your system memory that the program is allowed to use. Go to Edit > Preferences > Memory & Image Cache (**Figure 6.2**) and move the slider in the Physical Memory Usage box from the default of 50 percent to 65 or 70 percent. (Remember to change it back if you need to open several applications at the same time later on.)

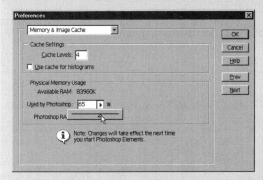

Figure 6.2 You can specify how much memory your editing program should use.

On the Mac Classic OS (System 9.22 or below), you can set how much memory an application can use and the minimum amount that it needs. With the application closed, select the application icon, and press Command-I (**Figure 6.3**). Change the preferred amount first, and then the minimum. You can't do this with OS X; it uses memory differently and doesn't have any Info boxes.

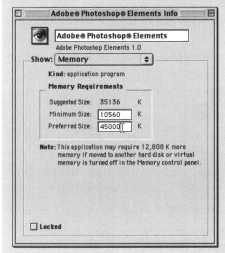

Figure 6.3 Change the memory requirement in the program's Info dialog box.

than try to create your own prints. You can send the service your files, and use its Web pages to share your work with others. Another plus in staying digital is that Internet sharing requires very little photo improvement, because lots of flaws aren't as obvious on screen as they would be in a full-color print. And you can manipulate a low-resolution file in the cheapest and easiest of programs. You only need a more powerful program if you plan to print large, full-color prints, or you want to experiment with photo collages or complex digital photo retouching.

In surveying software options from simplest to most extensive, we found dozens of possibilities. We'd love to talk about all of them, but then this book would be all about software instead of digital cameras and what you can do with them. So in this section we highlight programs that are popular, are proven, and in our estimation offer good tech support and/or good value. We concentrate on applications that offer downloadable trial versions. Every person has a different working process, so if you can play with software before you commit to buying it, you'll be happier in the long run.

Drop and Crop

If all you want is a foolproof way to make a simple correction and then share your photos, you many not need a real image editor at all. *Drop-and-crop* software, which lets you browse for or drag your images into a window where you can make simple cut-and-paste changes like cropping, will serve you nicely. The correction functions are automated to make it easy to fix your photos even if you have rudimentary computer or photography skills. And drop and crop is easy on your computer's memory and disk storage.

Don't expect this software to handle special tasks, however. It's better at organizing images than editing. For example, some services offer a "quick fix" button to optimize your photos. But any photo with serious problems, or shot under unusual conditions, will probably not improve with this automatic change.

Here are some online photo service sources with drop-and-crop photo editing options:

Picture It! (Windows)
www.photos.msn.com

This service offers the best combination of photo service and drop-and-crop software, but only for Windows users. This stripped-down version of Microsoft Picture It! performs a variety of fixes on your images, such as the Instant Fix (which makes one-click color and contrast corrections), red-eye reduction, and brightness and contrast correction. It also lets you add effects, such as applying a sepia tone (that brownish tint that makes a picture look antique) or changing a color photo to black and white. It even looks at the file resolution of images on your disk to tell you what you can successfully do with a photo before you upload it (**Figure 6.4**)—a handy device that saves you from uploading images you can't use for printing. For a fee, your picture can be the centerpiece of anything from a teddy bear to a T-shirt. The drawback: You must upload everything to the MSN site first and do all your editing there. If you have a very slow connection or decide to use the site during prime time, you can wait a long time to do very simple things. Cyndi waited five full minutes just to open a picture folder one Sunday evening—and she has broadband.

OfotoNow (Windows, Mac)
www.ofoto.com

You can download OfotoNow even if you aren't using the Ofoto service. It's easy to use, and since it resides on your computer, it doesn't depend on the speed of your connection or limit you to images that you've uploaded. Ofoto has red-eye reduction and standard zoom and cropping features. Less useful is its insistence that you save every change you make before you can make another one—awfully irritating when you have red eye on four faces and must save eight times before you're done. On the plus side, it reads the standard types of files that your camera uses for your photos, it works independently, and it's usable on both the Classic Mac and the Windows platforms.

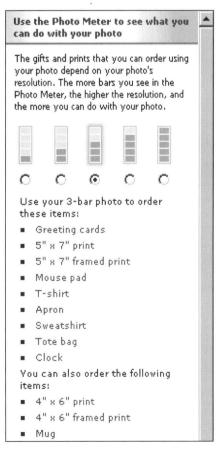

Figure 6.4 Even if you don't own Picture It!, you can join the photos.msn.com Web site and take advantage of some of its basic editing options.

iPhoto (Mac OS X)
www.apple.com

iPhoto is a terrific photo freebie, although like Ofoto's software, it's a bit of a stretch to call it an image editor. It offers effective red-eye reduction for most photos (it has problems with pictures in which the eye is so small that it's nothing but red eye) (**Figure 6.5**), as well as brightness and contrast options. It also provides image cropping and resizing and a quick button to turn your color photos into black-and-white ones. No question, iPhoto's strengths are really in its easy upload, image cataloging, and glorious printing options. Because iPhoto already has a database of USB cameras, you can plug your camera into your Mac without installing a single driver and all your images will automatically upload directly into iPhoto's cataloger. And nowhere else can a few minutes of work result in an inexpensive but beautifully bound, full-color book from your images that arrives within days of shooting your pictures.

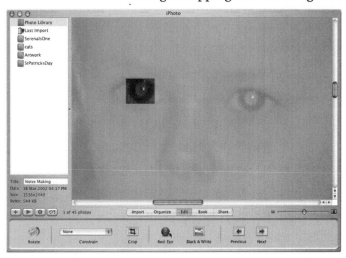

Figure 6.5 You can easily zoom up and select an eye to be fixed, although you'll need an eye like this one, that gives iPhoto enough information to work with. When you begin to drag your mouse over the area, the rest of the image fades down to make it easy for you to see your work. If you don't select quite enough of the eye, you can stretch the active area in any direction before you choose the Red Eye tool.

No, iPhoto doesn't have many editing tools. But with another download, from www.caffeinesoft.com, or the purchase of a new Macintosh, you can have PixelNhance. It's great freeware, with a cool and compact OS X interface that gives you photo-editing control of your pictures. With a quick setting in the iPhoto Preferences dialog box (**Figure 6.6**), it will take over seamlessly as iPhoto's photo editor every time you click iPhoto's Edit button. Although PixelNhance's photo-editing options are very good, there is no special setting for red eye, so you'll have to either change the Preferences setting back to the regular iPhoto editor every time you want to fix red eye or do all your red-eye fixes and image edits at once in a batch.

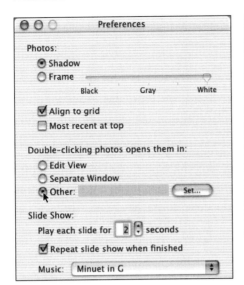

Figure 6.6 You can set any editing software (like PixelNhance or GraphicConverter) to take the place of iPhoto's rudimentary edit function by changing the Edit setting in the Preferences dialog box (left). When you select the Set button, you get a second dialog box where you can choose your desired program (right).

If you are a Windows user with iPhoto envy, Jasc After Shot for Windows offers many of the same functions of the iPhoto and PixelNhance combo at a reasonable price.

Image Editors

We recommend that beginners use a photo editor for most standard photo fixing. Image-editing software usually has too many options that you'll never use, and no helpers or templates for projects. In addition, many free and shareware image editors are optimized for posting pictures on the Internet and may not even be able to work with high-resolution JPEGs. That's OK if you don't expect to print your pictures, but most of us still do.

On the other hand, if you're good with a mouse or tablet, you'll have more manual control with an image editor. Image editors often have detailed controls for brightness, contrast, and color mix that can make up for the lack of a red-eye function. And if you want to get artistic, only an image editor with painting tools will give you all the options you need.

Freeware Image Editors

VCW VicMan Photo Editor (Windows)
Download from www.cnet.com.

We mention this program because it is hands-down the most popular image editor on the Windows platform. Photo Editor has a colorful interface and an abundance of filters for creating distortions and textures. It has an important feature for the beginner: multiple undos, unusual in free- or shareware. But despite its popularity, this is not the best tool for photo editing. Brightness, contrast, and saturation tools are all limited (**Figure 6.7**)—and you need these tools to be flexible to fix problems with color casts, over- or underexposure, and other lighting mistakes (see Chapter 8). On the other hand, you get a stable, easy-to-use program that fixes photos for Web use for absolutely nothing.

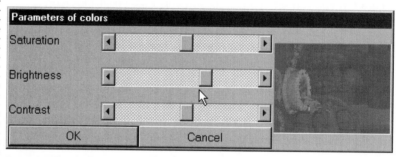

Figure 6.7 You'll discover that linear sliders (like these in Photo Editor) are not good tools for fixing a photo's brightness.

GIMP: Gnu Image Manipulation Program (Windows, Unix, Mac)
www.gimp.org

The GIMP was created in Unix as part of the GNU project, in which programmers create free software for public use. This version has been *ported* (meaning its code translated from the original platform to a different one) to Windows and the Mac OS X, and is not quite as stable as the Unix original. As a result, the GIMP's interface is a hodgepodge: It doesn't look like a Windows program, it doesn't have its own application window, and palettes float everywhere (**Figure 6.8**). But if you're looking for features, lots of filters, and power—and you don't want to pay for them— the GIMP could be your answer. The GIMP can't quite match Photoshop's dazzling array of functions, but it comes as close as a

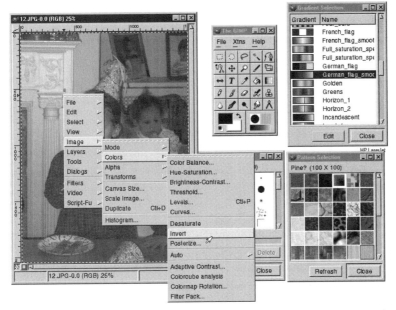

Figure 6.8 The GIMP (as its programmer refers to it) combines extremely powerful editing and creation tools with an unbeatable price. Of course, the GIMP is as quirky as it is powerful, as you can tell from its screen layout.

free program possibly could. It has a well-equipped toolbox and brush selection, as well as layers, several selection tools, and other tools critical to successful photo editing. What is doesn't have is a nice protective interface between you and its programming. In Unix and Mac OS X, you have to know how to compile programs just to install it. This is the perfect program for a computer genius with an urge for self-expression. It is not a good program if you are as new to computers as you are to digital photography

If you want to give the GIMP a try, The GIMP for Linux and Unix: Visual QuickStart Guide, *by Phyllis Davis, from Peachpit Press, is much easier to work with than the GIMP's own documentation.*

Staz Software FuturePaint (Mac)
www.stazsoftware.com

FuturePaint gives you an awful lot for a free program. Although you get only one level of undo (a little scary in image editing), you have excellent control over the most important editing features. The program interface looks like Photoshop's, with a similar arrangement of the most familiar tools (**Figure 6.9**). There are only a few filters, but they are all devoted to photo adjustments, particularly ones for color-related problems. In some ways this program represents the best of the sometimes wild and crazy world of freeware. The programmer is also the programmer of the FutureBasic programming language, and as such offers much of the hands-on responsiveness and personality of a program like the GIMP. But unlike the GIMP, FuturePaint is easy to use and reasonably well-behaved.

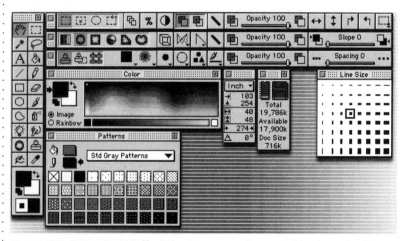

Figure 6.9 FuturePaint offers the Mac user dozens of tools and editing options.

Commercial Image Editors

Ulead® PhotoImpact® (Windows)
Download a 30-day trial version at www.ulead.com

PhotoImpact is such a large program because it's bursting with one-click enhancements, filters, and editing functions It does a great job of analyzing an image and recognizing similarities. In most programs, you'd have to create a mask to recolor the wall behind the cat (**Figure 6.10**) without also covering the rest of the image. PhotoImpact recognizes when a visual area should be treated like an object, not individual pixels. Novices with big dreams might find the answer to their prayers in this program. PhotoImpact will make your photos look good with-

Figure 6.10 PhotoImpact makes it easy to make big changes to an image in an instant.

out almost any effort on your part, yet unlike Microsoft's Picture It! it has enough manual tools that more experienced users won't feel frustrated when they want to take more control of the editing process.

MicroFrontier Color It!™ (Mac)
www.microfrontier.com

Color It! has been around for years and has a well-deserved following. If you work on an older Macintosh, this is a particularly good choice. It's gentle on system memory but gives great results nonetheless. In fact, it offers advanced options like masking, curves, and levels (see Chapter 8 for more on these tools) that you won't find in any other nonprofessional programs. You have a limited number of undos and no magic wand tool, but these are relatively small compromises for a great program.

Jasc Paint Shop Pro (Windows)
www.jasc.com

Paint Shop Pro started as a simple-to-use program for the average user, but by now it could be considered a professional image-editing package. Over the years, it has maintained its intuitive interface while gaining an impressive array of features, such as vector shapes, which essentially amount to an illustration program bundled into the image editor. Like Photoshop and Photo-Paint, it is both an image and photo editor, with red-eye removal and good control of color, brightness, and contrast. For the price, this is a hard program for a Windows user to turn down.

Photo Editors

If you are a digital camera owner who doesn't aspire to be an artist, you should concentrate on programs designed specifically for photo fixing. Although there are a few shareware photo editors around, the best options right now are commercial applications.

Adobe Photoshop Elements (Windows, Mac)
www.adobe.com

We're old hands at photography and photo editing, and Elements is the photo tool most like the professional Photoshop software we use for our own work. In fact, many of the screenshots in this book are from Elements. If you think you might someday want to move up to Photoshop, Elements is a terrific learning tool. It comes with a great help function that explains what you're doing and why you need to do it. Several important elements that are missing in Photoshop (like the red-eye reduction tool) have been added, along with a host of pre-made compound filter effects.

ArcSoft PhotoImpression™ (Windows, Mac)
www.arcsoft.com

Canon and several other camera companies include this software when you purchase their cameras, an extra bonus indeed. But even if you have to buy it, you'll get a good return on your small investment. This image editor is both easy to use and surprisingly versatile and powerful, with an interface that's attractive and intuitive. You can resize, fix red eye, and selectively retouch or apply effects. PhotoImpression has multiple levels of undo, and supports layers. Delightfully, this program was created by people with both taste and a sense of humor: The playful greeting card extras—frames, cutout shapes, pre-formatted scenes into which you can seamlessly insert a face— offer hours of fun even if you have no patience for detailed photo editing (**Figure 6.11**). Download a 30-day trial version of the more high-powered commercial package, Photo-Studio® for Windows or Mac OS X, at www.arcsoft.com.

Microsoft Picture It! (Windows)
www.photos.msn.com

Picture It! is ideal if you love doing home projects but don't want to devote your life to them. A photographer or computer whiz will probably find this program limited, but a home user new to photo editing will be happy and comfortable. Besides the obvious must-haves like red-eye reduction, it offers a single-click method to convert your photo to an ersatz charcoal drawing. There are a multitude of wizards for making every photo-based goodie you can imagine: calendars, greeting cards, stickers. And if that isn't enough, the Publishing Platinum version (the same price as Picture It! alone—go figure) includes a desktop-publishing program, so you can take the photos you're editing and place them right into a newsletter or flier.

Figure 6.11 PhotoImpression makes editing both fun and easy. You can easily make anyone into their fantasy...or nightmare.

GraphicConverter (Mac, Mac OS X)
www.lemkesoft.com

There isn't a perfect category for this great shareware program. We've put it here in the photo-editing section because it isn't an image editor or a free drop-and-crop. It performs a host of tasks that make it a favorite of photographers. It does excellent brightness and contrast repairs (**Figure 6.12**), creates slideshows, and even previews how a photo will look when viewed on a PC. And it's a terrific image organizer and catalog printer. GraphicConverter was originally created to convert one graphic file format into another, which it does efficiently. It converts all of the most popular file formats for easy editing and sharing of photos. It also converts

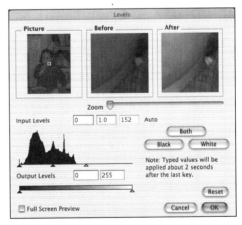

Figure 6.12 Although it approaches the task in a slightly different way, Graphic-Converter can equal the results of any commercial program, for a fraction of the cost. Its rendition of Levels (a key tool for any serious photo editor) makes it easy to fix photos that turn out too dark.

photos in batches, so if you have a pile of photos in RAW format that you need as JPEGs in a hurry, this is the tool for you. We can't recommend it highly enough for Macintosh users.

Professional Editing Software

Professional editing software combines all the features and functions you need for both image and photo editing, along with photo touch-up and professional printing options the average digital camera owner will never use or need to know about—not to mention all the third-party plug-ins and filters for doing everything from the sublime to the unnecessary. A novice could spend the next year doing nothing but taking digital photos and exploring a professional package's options.

Even if you think you need a professional toolbox, there are other issues to consider. Professional imaging software is not inexpensive, either to buy or to support. It requires space the size of the Taj Mahal on your hard drive, lots of RAM (usually a lot more than the package lists as a minimum), and a fast computer. All of these are worth the expense if your work requires it, but if you're doing photography purely for fun, you'll be better off with something more straightforward.

Adobe Photoshop (Windows, Mac)
www.adobe.com

As artists and designers, we both use Photoshop. Photoshop is an invaluable tool for us, but it is probably overkill for someone who is not (and does not aspire to be) a professional. Although there are competing products, Photoshop remains the commercial imaging standard.

Corel Photo-Paint® (Windows, Mac)
www3.corel.com

Photo-Paint covers a lot of the same ground as Photoshop, although it uses a completely different set of function names as well as a more Windows-like interface. It's still playing catch-up in the features race, but it's also arguably a little easier for a beginner to master. The Macintosh version is frequently one revision behind the Windows one.

Photos and File Types

7

Image files have different formats—and each format saves and archives information about that image differently. One picture, saved in two different formats, can look startlingly different. The result depends on each format's rules for interpreting image data.

If all you do with your digital photos is send them off for printing, you don't need to know about different file formats (also called *file types*). But if you plan to edit or resize them, or to use them for both printing and online display, a basic knowledge of file formats helps you avoid mistakes and maintain image quality.

Choosing an Image File Type

Before you take pictures with a traditional camera, you have to decide what type of film to use. You can choose print or slide film, black-and-white or color, film for bright outdoor use, film for long exposures, and even multipurpose film to cover a wide range of conditions. Once you've put the film in the camera, you're committed, because it's very hard (and in many cases, impossible) to roll exposed film back into its original canister, then roll it forward to the next unexposed area of film. That's why many professional photographers travel with different types of cameras loaded with different types of film.

With digital photography, you don't have to decide what type of film to use. One setting lets you go from the bright outdoors to low indoor light, or anything in between. But you may want (or need) to change the file type, either before you shoot, or before you edit. Like film types, file types are designed to let you do certain things very well—but not all things. A file type that produces wonderfully tiny files might be terrible for high-end printing.

The following is a tour through the types of files you might encounter with digital photography. A digital camera itself produces three file types: JPEG, TIFF, and RAW. RAW is a special case (see below), but JPEGs and TIFFs are frequently found on computers as well. Other file formats include those used for creating Web graphics and those that are *proprietary*—meaning they're created and owned by one company for use with its own software.

JPEG

Every digital camera uses this format as its default. Many digital cameras, in fact, only record images as JPEGs. *JPEG* stands for Joint Photographic Experts Group, and it's technically a mathematical formula for compressing images to make their file size smaller. JPEG was specifically designed to compress *continuous tone* images—so called because the image has no sharp edges where pieces of the picture start and stop. Photographs are continuous tone, as is a computer *color blend* (a smooth transition from one color to another) and some real-world artwork like watercolor paintings. On the other hand, pen-and-ink drawings and letterforms (which have more clearly delineated lines) are not continuous tone, so they don't convert to JPEG very well (**Figure 7.1**).

The people who created the JPEG format knew a curious fact about how humans see: Unlike other sharper-eyed animals, we don't notice small shifts in color as much as we notice shifts in brightness. And if we can't see the color changes, they might as well not be there. The JPEG formula analyzes the raw image the camera shoots and dumps the "invisible"

Figure 7.1 This piece of type from a graphic has been turned into a JPEG. As you can see, the original type on the right is clearly a solid color. On the left, after being saved as a JPEG, the type looks splotchy, with some places lighter than others.

data the human eye can't detect. That's why JPEG is called a *lossy* format, because data gets lost in the process. How much gets lost depends on the quality level you set.

You might think, "Well, if I can't see it, good riddance!" Not so fast. If you want to alter the image—make it bigger or smaller, or edit something in the image—you'll likely notice the loss. JPEG optimizes the image to look best at the size and resolution that were set when you shot the image. Change one of those parameters, and suddenly you might notice the errors you couldn't see before. So if you plan to resize and then print a picture, you'll want to minimize what gets thrown out.

Depending on its price and age, your camera gives you the option of shooting pictures at several JPEG quality levels. Frequently, you'll have the choice of Standard, Fine, and Superfine quality (**Figure 7.2**). Choose the finest setting, and you'll maintain the most raw image data in your JPEG. Keep in mind that the more image data you record, the bigger the file size for each picture.

Figure 7.2 Here's an example of the quality choices shown in one camera's menu: Besides TIFF, the options are SHQ (super-high quality), HQ (high quality), and SQ (standard quality).

TIFF

TIFF (Tagged Image File Format) is the oldest image format that's not specific to a type of computer, and it's still going strong. Some digital cameras give you the option of saving files in TIFF format rather than JPEG. If you want a picture with all its original depth of image intact, TIFF is a good choice. Professional photographers frequently save their images that way to maintain as much information for printing as they can.

The big problem with using TIFFs is...they're BIG. A high-quality JPEG that's about a megabyte in size will be at least several times that size if saved as a TIFF (**Figure 7.3**). As a result, you'll fit very few pictures on a Flash card. Even worse, the delay they cause during processing makes the normal digital camera shutter delay look inconsequential. A typical TIFF on a 3-megapixel camera can easily take 20 seconds to process—not exactly suitable for action shots, or even children's birthday parties.

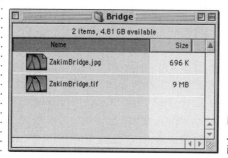

Figure 7.3 A reasonably sized JPEG file is much bigger once it's turned into a TIFF.

Is the quality difference worth the megabytes? For the average user, we don't think so. Very few of us are going to enlarge our photos to 13 x 18 inches and wallpaper our rooms with them; and at normal 4 x 6 sizes, you really can't tell the difference between a good JPEG and a TIFF. For blowing up a picture beyond snapshot size, you can always change your JPEG to a TIFF to help maintain quality. On the other hand, if you do expect to blow up your photos beyond 8 x 10, you might be better off spending the extra money for a camera that creates RAW photo images.

RAW

Unlike other file format names, RAW is not an acronym. RAW is exactly what it sounds like: unaltered, pristine image data.

It's what the camera actually sees when it takes your picture, translated into computer-language 1s and 0s. Even when you shoot in JPEG format, your camera's processor starts with this raw data and then massages it into the standard JPEG file format. But remember, once JPEG tosses out some data to make the image size smaller, the extra data is gone forever. On the other hand, if you shoot in RAW format, *you* get to make the decision about what to keep, and when. That means RAW format is ideal if you plan to enlarge the picture later, or if you want to minimize many cameras' tendency to oversharpen when they save a file as a JPEG.

RAW camera data produces file sizes that are only a little larger than a comparable JPEG, and tiny compared with the TIFF that would hold the same information. On a 2048 x 1536-pixel shot, a TIFF would be a gargantuan 9 MB. The RAW file holding the same information is only 1.7 MB.

So why not shoot in RAW format all the time? First, not all cameras even offer it as an option. Some companies offer it for their more expensive cameras but not for their beginner models—an incentive to upgrade if you like larger prints.

Second, unlike JPEGs and TIFFs, this file type isn't standardized across different cameras—RAW on a Canon is not the same as RAW on a Nikon. Each manufacturer sets its own standards, so you need special software from the manufacturer to be able to open and read a RAW file on your computer (**Figure 7.4**). Because the formats are different, software for one camera manufacturer won't necessarily work with that of another manufacturer; so if you have two cameras from different companies, you'll need to install both pieces of software.

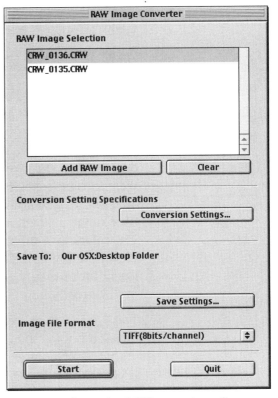

Figure 7.4 This is the RAW converter software utility that comes with Canon cameras.

We like using the RAW format for special shots, although we stick with JPEG at the High Quality setting (or Fine setting on some cameras) for most everyday shots.

System File Types

Macintosh and Windows computers allow you to read and create files even if you've never installed special software on them. That's because each operating system has a special file format that was either created or tailored to fit that system's needs. On Windows the format is BMP (short for *bitmap*); on a classic Macintosh it's PICT (short for *picture*). Mac OS X uses both the Adobe PDF format (slightly customized) and JPEGs. You wouldn't want to turn any of your photos into a BMP or PICT unless you were certain your final project would never be run on a different platform. These system file types are very low-resolution formats that are best used for making custom icons, screensavers, or other system-specific graphics.

Web Graphics Formats

Besides JPEGs, the other graphics formats you'll most frequently encounter on the Web are GIF and PNG.

GIFs (Graphics Interchange Format) are not supported in some free or shareware image editing programs because the format is owned by a company that charges a licensing fee to use it. Although there are occasional exceptions, by and large you don't want to turn your digital photos into GIFs. Just as JPEGs were created especially for photo-like images, GIFs were created to turn line art, text, and flat-color images into very small files suitable for modem transmission. GIFs can handle only 256 colors at a time, which is far less than even a low-resolution photograph needs. Photos that are changed into GIFs lose a lot of their transitional colors, leaving the photos looking like really bad 1960s poster art (**Figure 7.5**).

The PNG (Portable Network Graphics) format is much better for Web photos than GIFs. It doesn't limit the number of colors, so a PNG of a photo won't look much different than a JPEG would, despite the fact that it might actually be a smaller file. Web developers have been predicting for years that PNG would become the standard Web image file format, but GIFs

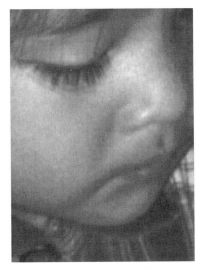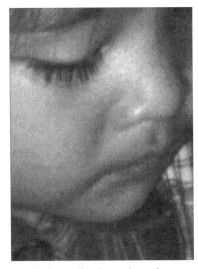

Figure 7.5 The original file, shown on the left, really degrades when you resave it as a GIF. Notice how rough and patchy the skin on the right has become.

and JPEGs remain more popular. PNGs are still not supported by some browser versions or any of the online photo services. As a result, we can't yet recommend that you use PNG for your digital photos.

Proprietary File Formats

In addition to the formats mentioned above, which are created and can be read by many different applications, there are also file formats that are created by specific applications and often can't be used by other applications. Both Photoshop and Photoshop Elements' PSD format is proprietary, but it's an exception to the rule. Not only is PSD usable by Photoshop and other Adobe applications, but many non-Adobe applications can open some PSD files as well. Whether or not a PSD file can be opened by a non-Adobe application depends on what version of Photoshop was used to create the file. As Photoshop has evolved over the years, it has become a more complex program. Many free or shareware programs can open PSD files created before Photoshop had layers, for example, but not Photoshop files created in later versions.

You may run into proprietary formats in image and photo-editing programs that use your images to create more complex projects with wizards or templates. Your original photo files (if you kept a copy of them) will still open in any program that can read them, but the new image you created from those photo files—say, for a calendar or T-shirt—may not.

Sometimes it can look like a file has turned into a proprietary format when it hasn't. Programs on Macs and PCs add information to files when you save changes using their functions. If you look at the file on your desktop, it may suddenly have a new icon. When you double-click on the new file, it only opens in the new program. But don't worry. If you want to use the file in a different program, launch that program first, then select File > Open and navigate to the file you want to open. Chances are pretty good that it will open, because the file format may still be JPEG underneath the icon change.

J

Ofotopicture

Changing an Image File Format

Although you can change just about any graphics file type into any other file type with the right software, some formats are more useful than others. When you change file type, you change the way the file's information is organized and saved. You can decrease an image's quality by changing its format. If the format you choose doesn't "know" how to hold onto some image information, changing the format can alter or delete some of the image data.

But there are several good reasons to change your file format. The most important is that JPEG, while a really useful format for many things, is a bad format for image editing. Every time you make changes to a JPEG file and resave it, the quality of the image gets worse, no matter what quality setting you choose. (See more about quality settings below.) In our opinion, one thing that distinguishes good editing software from bad is the ability to change a JPEG into a TIFF file—an excellent format for editing.

Save, and Save Again

If there is one critical piece of advice about image editing, this is it: **Never** edit the original file. Once you've changed the original data, you can never change it back again. If the file is your only copy, it's as if you had taken the original negative from a film and thrown it away.

Before you even open a file in an editing program, find it on your disk and make a duplicate of it. (On the Mac, that's Command-D; on the PC, use Ctrl-C to copy and then Ctrl-V to paste.) The copy will bear the word *copy* in its filename. This will make it less likely that you'll inadvertently replace the original.

As you edit, and especially before you make a big change, save your work in progress. You should do this even if the editing program you use allows you to make multiple undos, particularly if you may not have a lot of system memory and are working on an older computer. Saving versions ensures that you'll have less work to redo if your computer crashes or runs out of memory while you are working.

Use progressive numbering so you can keep track of your versions and delete them after you're finished. If your file is named Mary you can name the second copy Mary2. Unless you are very cramped for disk space, save at a couple of stages in your editing so you can go back to an earlier version if you do something you don't like (Uh oh, Mary looks dreadful with a moustache).

Don't confuse Save, Save As, and Save As a Copy, particularly if you are editing a JPEG. The Save command just inserts any changes you've been making into the existing file. If the existing file is your original shot, you've violated Rule #1, and lost the original picture file forever. The Save As command closes the file you have been working on without making any unsaved changes in it, then saves what you see on screen in the new file. Save As a Copy (if your program offers it as an option) is the best choice. It makes a copy of the file with all the changes you've made, just like a regular Save As, but it also puts the new copy on the disk and leaves the version you've been editing open for further changes.

To change a file's format, you need a program that can read and write both formats. Commercial image editors offer the broadest range of options, while drop-and-crop programs don't let you change file format at all. Before you buy or download a program, make sure it supports the file types you need. If you can't find that information for a program you've already downloaded, just create a new file and choose File > Save As. If the program supports more than one file

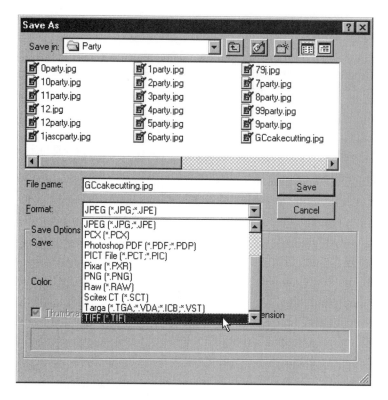

format, a drop-down menu in the Save As dialog box will display the choices, as seen above.

If you don't want to make any other edits, the process of simply changing a file format can be as easy as opening a file and choosing the new format from the Save As dialog box. But both TIFF and JPEG have variations that you need to select from before the format change will take effect.

You can't increase image quality after you've taken a photo. If you want an ultra-high-quality print, begin by shooting in TIFF or RAW format (whichever your camera supports). If you can only shoot in JPEG, choose your camera's Superfine setting.

TIFF Options

When you save a file and choose TIFF as the file format, the TIFF dialog box appears and offers two options. The first option is a set of radio buttons where you choose either a Macintosh or a Windows preview. You only want to change this radio button from its default setting if you need to transfer the TIFF file to a different platform to edit it. You may not be able to view and edit the file on the original platform otherwise. This option only affects the

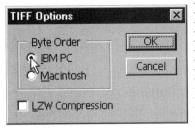

way the image displays onscreen, not the image information itself; so if your application can read both Mac and PC versions of TIFF (the way Adobe programs can), you can always change this setting without harming the file.

The second option in the TIFF dialog box is the LZW Compression check box that you can select to make the TIFF file more compact. Unlike the JPEG format, LZW compression doesn't throw out information. However, you won't see any reduction in file size with this setting unless large areas of your photo are exactly the same color (like a flat, solid-color box)— which is unlikely with a photograph. Frankly, we don't think it's worth bothering to select this option for photo editing.

JPEG Options

The JPEG Options dialog box that appears after you save your file as a JPEG is deceptively simple. In fact, the settings you choose here will greatly affect the quality of your image and what you can do with it. Although JPEG is a standardized format, the way different applications incorporate it is not. Different applications may present the same choices differently, with different results.

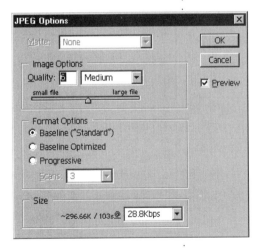

Quality

The most important choice is the Quality option. Quality is often confused with resolution, but they measure different things. Resolution is measured by the number of pixels in the picture; quality is how much color information JPEG compression retains. The lower the quality, the more changes take place.

Although JPEG quality is a continuous setting, like a volume knob, cameras and some software limits your quality options to fixed settings (usually three): low, medium, and high quality.

The different ways various programs implement their quality settings can create a lot of confusion. Adobe uses a quality scale from 0 to 12, with 12 being the highest quality and 0 the lowest. Other applications use a scale from 1 to 99 or 100. To further confuse matters, some programs use this scale to measure quality (with 100 being the best quality), while others use it to measure compression (with 1 being the least compression—and thus the best quality) (**Figure 7.6**).

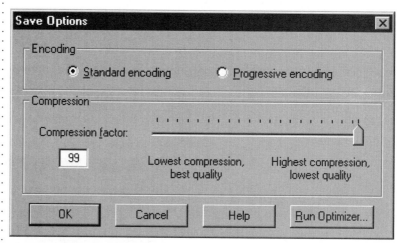

Figure 7.6 This application measures the highest quality as 1 and the lowest quality as 99.

In addition, these scales don't adhere to common standards. For example, the highest-quality setting in Jasc's Paint Shop Pro creates a file 400 KB smaller than does the highest quality setting in Photoshop Elements. Even worse, these settings don't correlate to the quality settings on cameras. A photo shot on a Canon S30 at Superfine quality, the highest JPEG compression available on the camera, ends up 200 KB larger when saved at the highest quality setting in Paint Shop Pro.

The quality setting you choose depends on what you're about to do with the file. To get a decent snapshot-size full color print on photo paper, your quality level shouldn't dip below 10 in Adobe programs and 75 or 80 in other programs (remember to reverse that number for programs that measure compression in percentages). You can often go as low as 3 (or 20 to 25 percent) on images that you'll post on the Web. Experiment to find what works best to your eye (**Figure 7.7**).

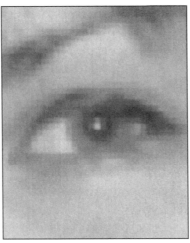

Figure 7.7 As you can see here, the images degrade more as you lower the quality setting. But remember, these pictures have been printed. On screen, you can get away with a fairly low-quality image and still have an acceptable picture.

Standard or Optimized Options

Your software may give you the option to optimize your JPEG. Optimizing makes your files smaller, but with a slight hit in quality. Many people swear that they can't see the difference, and on Web sites they are probably right. We don't recommend that you choose the Optimized option for JPEGs you plan to print. Any extra optimization could create added visual noise that will be noticeable in a print.

Progressive Option

This option is useful only if you want to show a large version of a photo on your Web site. If you select Progressive, the browser will load the photo in stages, beginning with a very low-resolution version of the picture, and adding definition and detail until the entire photo appears. Progressive JPEGs won't work in all browsers (or all image editors or readers), and they take up more storage space.

Image-Editing Basics

Image editing is easy to do—once you understand the basic concepts behind it. Many people who edit their photos start off enthusiastically, but soon become discouraged by the results. Everything looks great on screen, but when they print the picture or turn it into a coffee mug, the result looks like a first-grader came through with big, fat crayons and blunt scissors.

In this chapter, we orient you to the concepts behind image editing, so you'll understand what you can and can't do, and what's worth your effort. And we introduce image- and photo-editing tools that will help you get the most out of your photo-editing experience.

Knowing What to Fix

Just because your photos are editable doesn't mean that you can do everything with them (although you certainly can do a lot). Some problems are easy to determine and equally easy to fix. Red eye is one example. (You don't need to fix red eye by hand anymore, thanks to the push-button programs that do it so well.) Other problems, like a color shift or a fuzzy image, might be fixable with a recipe or wizard, but they could also require manual adjustment if you want them exactly right, rather than just OK.

Then there are the problems that aren't so easy to figure out: The image doesn't look quite right, but you don't know enough to know what's wrong and whether it can be fixed. Some image programs, like GraphicConverter or Adobe Photoshop Elements, offer you diagnostic tools to help determine what an image needs (**Figure 8.1**). If you look at an image in one of these tools and it improves as you experiment, you not only end up with a better image, but you learn what to fix when a future image needs help.

Figure 8.1 The Variations dialog box in Photoshop Elements lets you see how your photo will look before you make changes in color and brightness. Each time you click a picture, all of the variations update to show you the effect combined with others. So if you click the Lighter box and the More Green box, the Current Pick will show you the result.

Some other editing tasks aren't really problems with the image, which might be perfectly fine and well exposed. Issues like a facial blemish or *hot spots*—places that are much brighter than the rest of the image—may seem difficult to fix because they involve changing the image, but they're actually relatively easy to repair if you have the right tools and a bit of patience.

Consider the resolution and quality of the pictures you want to edit before you spend time editing them. As editing tasks increase in complexity from simple cropping (which you can do at any quality level) to retouching and collaging, you'll need more image information. The best candidates for complex editing are those images that were shot in RAW, TIFF, or JPEG Superfine. (See Chapter 7 for an explanation of these file formats.)

Most important, you must understand what is beyond repair. You can't fix a really low-resolution image; there's usually not enough image data to work with. You can't fix an image that is actually out of focus, no matter how much you try. If you used a flash and an object is completely washed out, no amount of editing will bring it back. And an image with multiple difficult problems, each of which might be reparable individually, may just take too much time to be worth the effort.

Image-Editing Tools

Every program that offers editing tools takes a slightly different approach to the editing process, although many share the same vocabulary and icons. Bear in mind that each program arranges its tools somewhat differently. Although many programs follow the Photoshop format of combining a toolbox, menus, and palettes, most of the photo-editing programs with image-editing tools (like ArcSoft's PhotoImpression) do not. They tend to organize their tools differently and frequently use different icons. Fortunately, once you learn the basics with one program, it's pretty easy to match up those tools with similar ones in a new program.

Before you start editing, make sure that the program you plan to use actually does offer the tools you'll need. Don't assume. Check the program first, particularly if it's a photo editor. For example, Microsoft's Picture It! allows you to make many image changes, but only through its system of wizards. Wizard programs aren't good tools for repairing faces or backgrounds, and they're quite limited in correcting brightness, contrast, and similar problems. They're much better for projects (see Chapter 12).

Selection Tools

A full range of selection tools is key to good image editing, because you need a way to tell your program exactly what you'd like to change. These specialized tools help you select exactly the right portion of the image. You can select by drawing, by clicking, or with keyboard shortcuts and menus. You can specify a small area of an image, a range of colors, or in some cases objects.

A

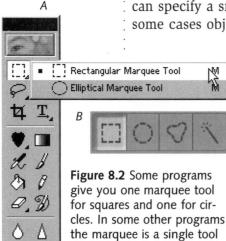

B

Figure 8.2 Some programs give you one marquee tool for squares and one for circles. In some other programs the marquee is a single tool with variations for different types of geometric shapes.

At the very least, you need three basic selection tools for image editing: the marquee, the magic wand, and the free-form tool. The marquee selects geometric areas: squares, rectangles, circles, and ovals (**Figure 8.2**). The magic wand tool selects areas of similar color—it's a good tool for selecting an object along with its shadows and bright spots (**Figure 8.3**). The free-form tool lets you select by drawing around specific areas you want. It's good for selecting irregular shapes that are not all the same color (**Figure 8.4**). A professional image editor adds a variety of other selection tools and functions to the mix: a way to select things by their edges, a way to enlarge a magic wand's area by increasing the range of color similarity, and a more precise version of the free-form tool.

In most programs, you can add to an existing selection by holding down the Shift key while you click a different area.

Red-Eye Reduction

Although many digital cameras have a red-eye-reduction function (see Chapter 4), it's not foolproof. You'll frequently get red eye in your photos even if you use it. Because this problem is so prevalent, all photo editing software offers some type of red-eye-reduction tool.

Figure 8.3 Photoshop's Magic Wand tool is good for selecting large, continuous-tone areas that have variations of the same basic color—like the sky.

Figure 8.4 Only a free-form selection tool could possibly grab the complex combination of color and form of this sherbet glass. Cyndi used Elements' precise lasso tool, the Polygon Lasso, to make the selection outline.

Red-eye-reduction tools work by recognizing the specific shade and intensity of red that reflects back from the pupil, removing the color, and then darkening the area. These are all things that you can do by hand (and professional Photoshop users used to), but why should you? Cyndi has tried dozens of programs, from the simplest drop-and-crop to the most complex (**Figure 8.5**), and finds that most do at least an adequate job for most repairs. The best are so perfect it's almost scary. She has almost completely sworn off hand-editing red eye.

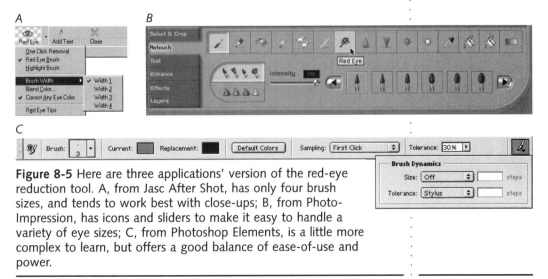

Figure 8-5 Here are three applications' version of the red-eye reduction tool. A, from Jasc After Shot, has only four brush sizes, and tends to work best with close-ups; B, from Photo-Impression, has icons and sliders to make it easy to handle a variety of eye sizes; C, from Photoshop Elements, is a little more complex to learn, but offers a good balance of ease-of-use and power.

Red-Eye-Reduction Hints

Although red-eye-reduction tools can give pretty impressive results, it's still possible to get a less-than-perfect result. Here are tips for getting it right every time:

- Don't fix red eye from a distance. Zoom the image up as close as you can before it breaks up into jagged pixels.

- Be careful to select only the pupil area itself, not the lid or whites. Most red-eye tools desaturate (eliminate color) when they are run over any portion of the image that has red in it.

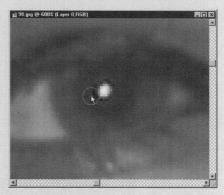

- Some red-eye-reduction tools also do a nice job of improving bloodshot eyes in close-ups. If your red-eye-reduction tool is applied with an adjustable-size brush, choose a smaller brush and run it lightly over the white part of the eye.

- Red-eye reduction works best if the subject is close to the camera or the picture was shot at a very high resolution. But if there aren't enough pixels that the program can identify as part of the eye, the tool can make the image worse.

A few things distinguish a good red-eye tool from one that's just OK. You should be able to apply the tool with a brush, rather than select the area with a marquee tool or one that draws a box around the eye. Geometric selection tools are less precise and don't always work on low-resolution images or when the person is shot at a distance. Brush sizes should be adjustable to correct red eye even in a small or low-resolution image (**Figure 8.6**). And applying the tool should make it easy to remove the redness without affecting portions of the eye that aren't red. A good red-eye tool should not just desaturate; it should be discriminating.

Red-eye correctors also work on some animal eyes, but only if the animal's eye reflects back red, not some other color. Cats, for example, can reflect the flash's light back as green or yellow.

A

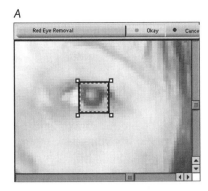

B

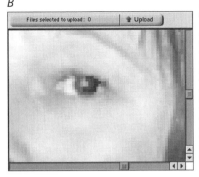

Figure 8.6 Ofoto's red-eye reduction is applied by drawing a box around the eye area—a method that's imprecise. In this image, which was shot at low resolution, the eye is distorted when the red-eye-reduction tool is used. It was impossible to get the box small enough to exactly encircle the center of the eye.

Hue, Contrast, and Brightness

Although many programs separate these three concepts into individual tools, you really can't talk about one of them in isolation, because a change in one affects the others.

On the computer, as in real life, *hue,* or color, is a rainbow continuum, as one shade blends gently into another. But the computer keeps track of these colors in three primary hues (red, green, and blue), which it organizes in color spaces called *channels*. If you eliminate one color channel of the three, the image will look like you applied a photographic filter to it. It will shift colors and look flatter and more garish. If you eliminate color from all three channels completely, the picture will go from color to black and white—in other words, it will *desaturate*. If you increase or decrease one channel just a little, you can frequently repair color shifting in an image that wasn't shot in outdoor daylight.

Tools that shift hue are variously called Color Cast, Color Balance, Hue/Saturation, Color Correction, or Curves. Some of them are sliders, with one color at the left end and another at the right. Sliders are easy to understand, but tools with linear controls seldom give great results in color and brightness editing. Other tools, like Photoshop's Curves, are more complicated to use and understand but give better results when you finally master them. Jasc's Paint Shop Pro approaches the problem in a novel way that's somewhere between sliders and curves in complexity, but often gives good results (**Figure 8.7**).

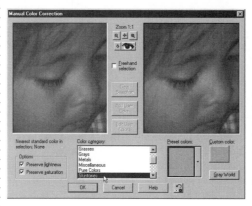

Figure 8.7 Jasc's Paint Shop Pro lets you select an area and use it to optimize the entire image based on presets for typical objects. In this example, we're color correcting by setting the image to the corrected skin tones.

You'll frequently see a slider tool called Brightness/Contrast. These two types of changes are combined because they're similar computer functions. The computer determines a pixel's shade (how light or dark it is) on a scale of 0 (black) to 255 (white). Adding numbers increases brightness, subtracting decreases it. If you add numbers throughout the image, you'll make the photo brighter. If you add too much, all the colors will wash out. If you make the numbers more extreme in either direction (darker pixels lower, lighter pixels higher), you'll increase contrast (**Figure 8.8**).

Figure 8.8 We've greatly increased the image contrast on the left and the brightness on the right.

Photoshop Elements' Fill Flash tool mimics the effect of using a fill-flash function on a camera. The image brightens, but not evenly. Bright areas brighten a little more, but the most dramatic brightness change is in the shadows. It's a wizard that lets you do in one step what would otherwise require fine adjustment and knowledge of levels.

There is a connection between color and changes in brightness. Of the three primary colors, blue is less bright overall than are red and green. So if you change the amount of a color in an image, you may also end up making it look brighter or darker. That's one of the reasons why slider tools are a little limited for correcting brightness. They don't usually allow you to change red, green, and blue individually. And even if they have separate sliders for each hue, you can't apply changes differently in dark and light areas. More professional image- and photo-editing programs offer a Levels tool as well as simple sliders to address these needs

Levels

The Levels dialog box is a special tool for fixing brightness and contrast. It almost always works better than a simple brightness/contrast slider (**Figure 8.9**). A Levels tool allows you to manually adjust an image to fit your aesthetic sense, or your memory of the scene when you took the picture. It allows you to vary the tonal values individually in the dark, light, and middle tones of an image, making pictures clearer, crisper, and more vibrant. Any levels tool worth its salt has all of these features: a *histogram* (a graph of how brightness is distributed in an image), *input* and *output* sliders, a way to set *white point,* and a preview big enough to show the result of your proposed change.

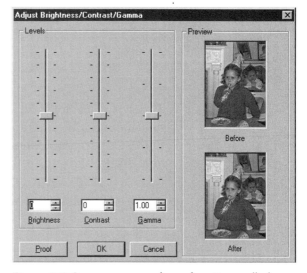

Figure 8.9 Some programs have functions called levels, but they are more like slider tools because they lack white point or other functions. This dialog box appears when you click the Levels button in ACD Systems' FotoCanvas™ editing program.

Figure 8.10 shows the Levels dialog box in Photoshop Elements. This levels tool allows you to change the brightness and contrast selectively for the different color channels. The histogram is a graph showing how each of the 256 possible pixels shades is distributed in your image. The taller the line at a given pixel shade, the more pixels there are at that shade. The histogram in this dialog box indicates that the picture is too dark.

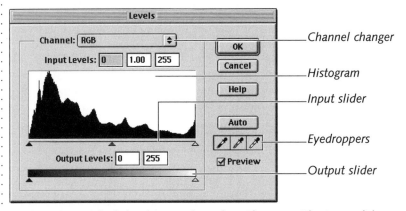

Channel changer

Histogram

Input slider

Eyedroppers

Output slider

Figure 8.10 Levels dialog box in Photoshop Elements. The input slider increases contrast when you move the arrows into the center. The output slider decreases contrast. Eyedroppers allow you to set the white, black, or midtone gray point of an image.

The best levels tools let you make changes on each color channel individually. Some programs that provide a full-featured levels tool are Photoshop and Photoshop Elements, the GIMP, and Paint Shop Pro. Although the Levels dialog box can seem daunting at first, once you get the hang of the tools they are relatively easy to control.

If you don't have levels, there may be an "instant fix" or "quick fix" setting in your software that sets levels automatically. If you do have a levels setting, look for an automatic levels setting as well. The quality of your result will vary according to the cleverness of the program. Sometimes the automatic result is so good that you don't have to use Brightness, Contrast, or levels at all. The less work you have to do on an image, the better.

Curves

Only the most sophisticated editing programs have a Curves dialog box (unlike levels, which crops up in some fashion in the majority of programs). This isn't surprising, since using color curves for anything but a wild effect involves patient experimentation; you have an infinite number of ways to define a color curve in a channel. Curves allow you to apply a change in contrast unequally in an image (**Figure 8.11**). By bending the straight line outward, you lighten the midrange shades without changing the darkest and lightest areas of the image. Bend the line inward, and you darken the midtones the same way. Cyndi loves working with curves, but doesn't recommend that you start your image-editing experience by trying to master them. Most, if not all, of the adjustments you'll want to make to your photos can be done perfectly well using levels.

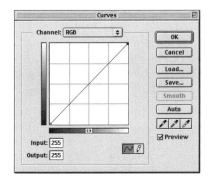
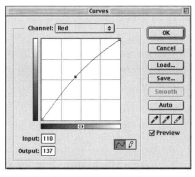

Figure 8.11 Adjusting curves is a more professional way to color correct an image. On the left is the default curve setting. On the right, Cyndi is increasing the amount of red in an image, mostly in the middle tones, by curving the line outward from the center. If she curved the line inward, she'd decrease red instead.

Dodge and Burn

Sometimes the area you want to darken or lighten is small, and using any of the tools that change brightness throughout the image doesn't work. Look in your software for the Dodge and Burn tools. Because they use the same technique applied for different purposes, these two tools are usually grouped together—sometimes as one tool, sometimes as part of a group of toning or retouching tools.

The terms are taken from the old days when images were fixed in the darkroom and refer to techniques for concentrating or blocking light. The Dodge tool lightens and the Burn tool darkens. Unless you're editing a black-and-white photo, you may find that these tools do too much too fast. You'll find them much more useful if your editing software lets you apply them at different transparencies (so they have a slower, smaller effect) or with different blending modes (a primarily Photoshop and Photoshop Elements term for different ways to combine tools and effects and to merge images).

Layers

Many editing programs have a layer function. A *layer* is a clear overlay on top of an original image. Depending on the program, you can have a limited number of layers or an infinite number.

Every empty layer is perfectly transparent, like a piece of clear acetate. When you put a picture (or part of a picture) on a layer, it covers whatever is directly beneath it, but lets the rest of the lower layers show through (**Figure 8.12**). Some programs let you vary the amount of transparency of the images on each layer. When an upper layer is made partially transparent, you can see the layer beneath. How well you see lower layers depends on how you set the layer's opacity—from 0%, which

Figure 8.12 The Layers palette, in the front, shows that the white text is on a separate layer from the photograph. The water shows through around the type instead of being blocked by the rectangular text box because the layer the type is on is transparent. Only the type is opaque.

is completely transparent, to 100%, which is completely opaque (**Figure 8.13**). One of the best ways to use layer transparency is to combine two or more photos together seamlessly for artistic effect.

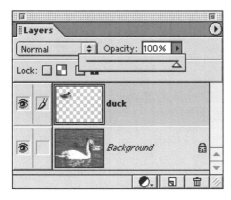

Figure 8.13 Set the opacity to determine how much of your lower layers should show through the ones on top.

Layers are versatile. You can make changes on one layer without affecting any other layers. They also let you duplicate parts of one image and add them into another (**Figure 8.14**).

Figure 8.14 The original picture had one fewer duck than you see in this one. Cyndi selected this duck from a different photograph and copied it into the swan picture, then used Elements' Paintbrush tool to help the duck blend into the swan photo.

Both Photoshop and Photoshop Elements have adjustment layers, which allow you to apply additional changes to a layer temporarily. That way, you can try out a major change before you commit to it, and compare the results of one change with another by turning layers on and off (**Figure 8.15**).

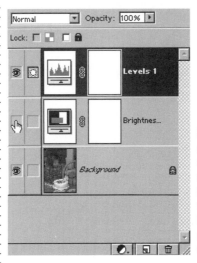

Figure 8.15 You can create two adjustment layers, one that changes the brightness of an entire image, for example, and the other that changes brightness through levels. By turning one layer on and the other off, you can view the differences between the two adjustments.

Using layers tends to significantly increase your file sizes. Each layer is potentially another complete image with the same dimensions of the original, so simply adding a layer to a file, even a layer with nothing on it, will make the file expand (**Figure 8.16**). To manage this problem, most programs allow you to *flatten* layers when you are done with them. Flattening merges all the visible layers into one layer again.

Figure 8.16 The swan image has two layers on top of the original, which was a 9 MB TIFF file. The two layers add 2.8 MB to the size of the file, even though one layer only has a line of type, and the other layer only has one duck.

Masks

A *mask* is a selection layer that protects an area of your photo from changes. In programs like Paint Shop Pro, you can turn a selection that you created with the selection tools into a mask, then save it for future editing tasks. For example, sometimes you begin to edit a photo after having spent a lot of time using the selections tools to define an area. Saving a selection as a mask lets you pick up where you left off without having to start selecting from scratch. Masks hide parts of an image from an editing tool while you work on areas you want to change (**Figure 8.17**). Using a mask you can, for example, merge the front image of one photo with the background of another, add an effect only to a background, or touch up one part of an image without worrying about making a mistake that will affect the larger image. Masks are also very useful for making projects. If you make a heart-shaped mask, for example, you can use it to create a Valentine's Day card with the image as a picture in the middle, and a solid color and type on another layer.

Figure 8.17 This mask protects the rest of the image while you edit the bird in the middle.

Since the whole purpose of a mask is to protect one part of a photo while you're editing another, any program that doesn't have selection tools doesn't have masking (or, most probably, layers) either. The better the selection tools, the better your masks, and therefore the better your editing is likely to be.

Cloning

A cloning tool (known as the rubber stamp tool in some programs) lets you copy pixels from an image and use it somewhere else in the same or another image. It's a painting, not a selection, tool, so you don't pick up an entire area all at once the way you would with cut-and-paste. You tag a tiny group of pixels (called the *sample*) and use the cloning tool to brush them into your target area, replacing the existing pixels in that portion of the target (**Figure 8.18**).

Figures 8.18 To remove the wires that mar this picture, we cloned pieces of the sky and tree using unaligned samples to pick up sky, then branches, to fill in the gaps realistically.

Sounds easy to do, but it's even easier to end up with fake-looking images. Part of the problem can be the tool. Simple image-editing programs can't refine the cloning options. But better programs add all or some of these possible refinements: the size and type of brush; transparency, and how a transparent sample blends with the target; and how you access the sample in the target image. The sample and the clone can be *aligned* (also called *continuous*), so that the first image is revealed as you paint over the second one; or the sample and clone can be *nonaligned,* where you treat the sample like a paint bucket, and "dip" into the same sample to paint different target areas (**Figure 8.19**).

Figure 8.19 To make an exact duplicate of an object, you align the sample and the original.

Most simple clone tools have a wide, hard brush, and can only paint continuously. This combination is good for replacing a big section of an image (like painting in a new background or repairing the look of a flat surface), but such a tool is too crude to easily edit out complex areas or make delicate repairs (**Figure 8.20**).

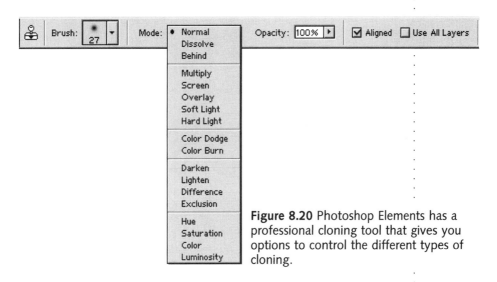

Figure 8.20 Photoshop Elements has a professional cloning tool that gives you options to control the different types of cloning.

When cloning between two images, the two images must be the same approximate size and resolution. Test how well they match by pasting a small selection from one image onto the other. If the size of the pasted piece is too big or small, you will have to adjust one image before you proceed.

Cropping

Every program offers a cropping tool. Cropping tools allow you to select a rectangular area on the screen and cut away anything outside that selected area. A good cropping tool should give you two ways to crop: by choosing a specific dimension (like 4 x 6 inches for a standard print), or by drawing a rectangle to describe the area you want—even if that area isn't a standard size. A really good cropping tool will let you adjust that rectangle on screen instead of making you draw it again if you need to adjust your selection before cropping (**Figure 8.21**).

Figure 8.21 Photoshop Elements allows you to easily adjust the position of the crop outline, as well as its length and width.

Although the cropping tool is simple to learn and use, it shouldn't be the first tool you reach for when you're editing a photo. Cropping deletes information from an image. If you crop before you change the print resolution and size, for example, you've effectively sliced away pixels...not the best move if you plan on making any other changes to the image. See the sidebar "Making Multiple Image Corrections" on page 136 for hints on when to crop.

In using the cropping tool, you should consider the same issues you would in shooting a good photo to begin with. For a refresher course on how to compose a good image, see Chapter 3.

Sharpening

In sharpening, the computer finds *edges*—image areas with a fair amount of contrast in brightness or color—and then emphasizes that contrast. Most people misuse sharpening effects, trying to fix unfixable fuzzy images. Sharpening doesn't clarify an out-of-focus picture. Rather, it's most effective when a picture is basically OK but could benefit from a slight increase in clarity, like right after you've resampled. The sharpen tool sees every place where there is a difference in the color of adjoining pixels as an edge, and it creates patterns that distort the edge in order to heighten the differences—rather than actually sharpening the image.

There are several sharpening options. A regular sharpen tool (Elements' Sharpen/Sharpen More is a good example) simply exaggerates the differences it finds between any darker and lighter areas. We don't recommend it unless you want a distressed effect. Repeated sharpening eventually leads to objects with dark edges that look fake. In **Figure 8.22**, the strange patterns on the child's face are called *artifacts*, and are caused by individual pixels being sharpened next to other individual pixels that should blend gently into each other. Better sharpen tools sharpen the edges while also gradually blending one edge color into the other.

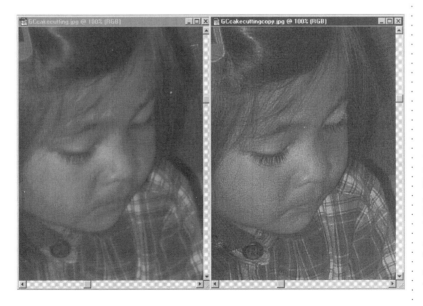

Figure 8.22 Look at the difference between the original image on the left, and the sharpened image on the right. The image on the right is sharper, but the texture of the child's face is somewhat pebbled.

There are two tools we recommend for sharpening. The first is Sharpen Edges, which you'll find in Photoshop and Photoshop Elements, as well as in Ulead's PhotoImpact. Unlike the regular Sharpen tool, it looks for distinct differences between pixels and sharpens only when it finds them. As a result, pictures usually look sharper without the ugly artifacts (**Figure 8.23**).

Figure 8.23 In this photo, Cyndi applied Sharpen Edges to enhance the difference between the bridge cables and the sky beyond them.

The second tool, Unsharp Mask, is a little more complicated to explain and use. The name is a strange leftover from the days when sharpening was done in the darkroom. Unsharp Mask produces a high-contrast sharpened edge that blends down gently to the two edge colors. The effect is sharpness without distortion. Many applications, from the GIMP to Photoshop Elements to ColorIt, offer Unsharp Mask.

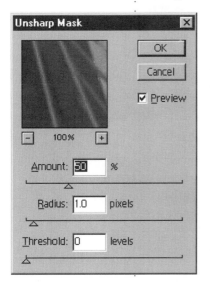

Unsharp Mask has three parameters you can change. The most important by far is Radius, which controls how wide an area of pixels will be affected. If you've ever used a painting tool on the computer, you know that you can change the thickness of the brush for different purposes. Changing Radius is like changing your brush width. The larger the radius value, you more area you sharpen. But if you choose too large a value, you'll over-sharpen and get artifacts just like you would with the regular sharpen tool. How large a radius you set depends on the resolution of your image. The higher the resolution, the larger the radius can be without distortion. Even with Superfine resolution from your camera, your radius shouldn't usually exceed 1.5 (**Figure 8.24**).

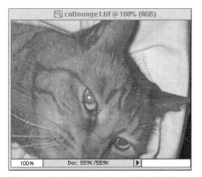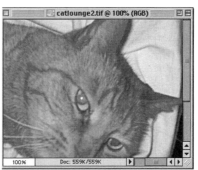

Figure 8.24 The cat on the left was sharpened with a radius of 1, and the other with a radius of 2. Notice that while the left image is crisp and clear, the image on the right is distorted. The cat's fur looks stiff and spiky, and the folds in the fabric are overly dark and dramatic.

After Radius, you set Amount. Imagine two pixels, one representing your son's lacrosse shirt, the other the blue sky behind him. Unsharp Mask increases the contrast between them for sharpness. Amount determines how much it increases the contrast. It's better to start lower and increase than to overdo the amount. Cyndi starts at around 50% for a Fine image, and increases from there if needed.

Threshold is what prevents you from sharpening tiny skin tone variations into ugly artifacts. It determines how different two pixels have to be from each other before sharpening takes places. The bigger the number, the more different two pixels have to be. There is no fixed number for this setting, because it's so dependent on the nature of your image. But anything over 8 or 9 is no help at all, because the number of pixel differences is so large that almost no sharpening will take place (**Figure 8.25**).

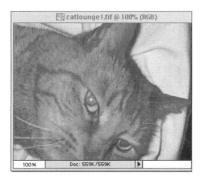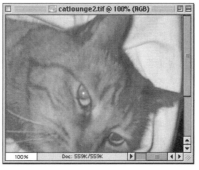

Figure 8.25 These images both had a radius setting of 1 and an amount of 100%, but the one on the left has a threshold of 1, and the one on the right a threshold of 8. As a result, the one on the right hasn't been sharpened at all.

Changing Resolution and Size

Not all editing software will let you manually change your resolution. In fact, most of the photo-editing software that's bundled with cameras won't. And if you're using wizards and preformatted projects, the software you use will make decisions for you.

But if you want to enjoy the full range of options your digital camera offers, you'll have many occasions when you'll want or need to manually change your resolution. If you want to place a photo in a desktop-publishing program, use it for an ad, print it on a desktop photo printer, or in fact do anything that involves printing the file out or giving it to someplace other than a photo-developing company for printing, you'll be interested in reading this section.

We've combined resolution and size changes, because in digital editing one can affect the other.

Changing Print Resolution and Size

Most cameras use the onscreen standard resolution of 72, which sounds low quality if you know a little about resolution. But there is a big difference between image resolution, which is determined by the number of pixels in an image, and print resolution, which is determined by how those pixels are organized. Right out of the camera, a high-quality image's resolution may be 72, but its print dimensions are enormous (**Figure 8.26**). Fortunately, print resolution can be

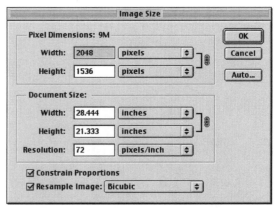

Figure 8.26 Yikes! Look at the document size in Photoshop Elements' Image Size dialog box. Imagine trying to print a 28 x 21-inch image on your color printer. You'll definitely need to adjust your document size before you can make a print of this image.

changed without affecting the actual image resolution. All you have to do is reorganize all of those pixels to increase the print resolution and decrease the print area.

If you're not using Photoshop or Elements and you want to change resolution, look for Image or Image Size in the menu bar. A dialog box that offers these options should be available.

As you can see in the dialog box, it's possible to change print and image resolution separately. If you change image resolution independent of the width and height, however, you'll degrade the image quality.

To avoid this result when you resize for printing, you'll want to prevent the program from resampling the file. *Resampling* changes the pixel dimensions. It examines a file and recalculates color and brightness for every pixel. Pixels get lost, added, or changed in the process. When you resize the document dimensions for printing, you don't want to change any pixels. You just want them organized a little differently. If you uncheck Resample Image, you lock the resolution and the dimensions together, so that anything that changes one is reflected in the other (**Figure 8.27**). This keeps the image quality from being degraded. Notice that when you uncheck Resample in the Image Size dialog box in Photoshop Elements, the upper set of pixel dimensions, which represent your camera's resolution, are no longer changeable. This is a visual clue to reassure you that you won't lose any resolution when you make your document size changes.

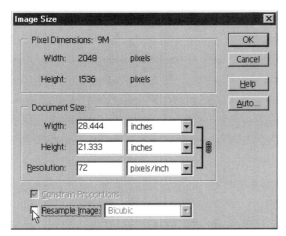

Figure 8.27 The Resample Image option ties pixel dimensions to document size, so changing one also changes the other.

Now, change any of the dimensions to your target, and all will adjust proportionally the way our example has (**Figure 8.28**).

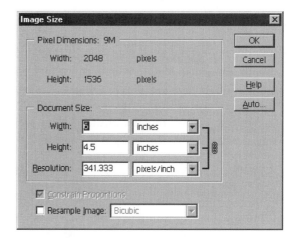

Figure 8.28 By changing the width to 6 inches, we automatically change the print size and resolution without changing the actual file resolution.

If the program you're using doesn't have a Resample function to uncheck, look for the option to Constrain Image Size. That's the opposite of resampling, so if you select it you'll preserve your image resolution.

Changing Image Resolution and Size

Sometimes you must change image resolution. If you've shot a picture at high resolution that you want to both print and put on a Web site, you need two versions. The second has to be at a much lower resolution or it will take forever to download for viewing. Thus, if we want a Web version, we leave Resample checked in the dialog box.

The only way to change the image resolution up or down is to resample. Since image resolution is determined by the number of pixels in a file, when you resample to decrease resolution, pixels get discarded. If you resample to increase resolution, pixels get invented to take up the new space through interpolation (essentially, by guessing according to certain rules). Once you've resampled up or down, the image has changed. Discarded pixels can't be recovered (another good reason to always have a copy of the original picture stashed away). If you try to upsample (resample up) an image that you've downsampled (resampled down), you just get an ugly picture.

There are two ways to resample. You can change just the pixel dimensions or you can change the print dimensions (**Figure 8.29**). In both cases, the width and height of the pixel dimensions will change. That's because, when you resample, you are asking the image-editing program to alter the image. If the dimensions are decreased, the file gets smaller and pixels are thrown away. If the dimensions are increased, the file gets larger as the program "guesses" where to add pixels.

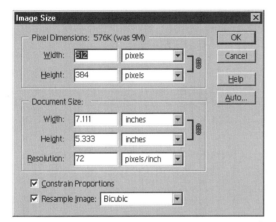 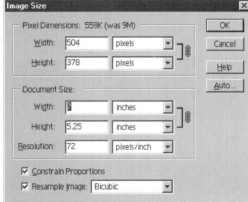

Figure 8.29 When you resample, you can simultaneously change the size of the file, the dimensions of the onscreen image, and the dimensions of the printed image; or you can leave the printing dimensions alone.

In addition, when you increase the pixel dimensions, the size of the image onscreen increases.

Resampling is often most successful if you change the pixel dimensions in evenly divisible numbers, so that there are fewer fractional pixels for the program to delete. If your image width is 2048, for example, changing it to 1024 may give better results than changing it to 999.

Proportions and Aspect Ratio

If you are resampling an image, you'll often also have the option to Constrain Proportions or Maintain Aspect Ratio. These are exactly the same thing. The aspect ratio is the proportion of width to height of a photo. For example, a 4 x 6-inch print has a 2 x 3 aspect ratio. So does a 2 x 3-inch or 3 x 4.5-inch print. If you don't constrain proportions, the program will change these dimensions rather than throw out or interpolate pixels when resampling. There is no case we can think of in which you would want to do this, because it will distort your image like a funhouse mirror, making things in the picture appear wider or narrower than they really were.

Final Touches

If you want to make your pictures feel more finished, you can add a frame—a nice touch for a Web site, or to set off a picture that you're putting in the family newsletter. And a caption can help you explain the story behind the picture.

Adding a Border

Almost every photo-editing program has some function for adding a border, usually tucked away in the Effects section. Some do all of the work for you by offering a selection of frames that become part of your image. As you might expect, there are usually several frames to choose from in a program with a framing wizard.

Most image editors, on the other hand, have either no frame tools or extremely limited ones. If you've been working with an image editor that has no border options, you can approach the project in two ways. The easiest is just to enlarge the canvas area (the dimensions of the working area, rather than the dimensions of the picture itself). Then all you have to do is fill the blank area with the color of your choice. If you want a more expressive border, you can select that section of the image, and use one of the program's special effects (**Figure 8.30**).

Figure 8.30 We applied the Gold Sprinkles effect in Elements to this image's border area.

Adding a Caption

There are two ways to add a caption: on top of the image, and to the side of it. All image editors, and some photo editors, have a text tool. If you decide to add text to the image, make sure that you leave this step for the very end of your editing process, when all your changes have been made, including any changes in resolution. Text looks strange when it loses resolution. It gets fuzzy and distorted, and will distract from your image instead of complementing it.

If all you want to do is label a picture with its filename when you print it, you might find that your software has a Caption function hidden away in the File or Print menu. In Elements, there's a File Info dialog box inside the File menu. If you select Caption in the Output section of the Print Preview box, anything you type there will print out.

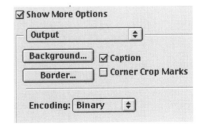

In addition, most photo management software, like iPhoto and Jasc After Shot, allows you to create a caption name for a picture to help you identify it. See Chapter 5 for more about Apple's iPhoto and its image cataloging and management functions.

Making Multiple Image Corrections

The order in which you edit your images is important. If you begin with the least destructive changes and work toward the most critical ones, you'll maintain the best quality in your photos and be able to recover more easily if you make a mistake along the way. Some edits simply must be done last to get acceptable results. For example, if you downgrade the quality of your JPEG too early in the process, you won't have enough image data to make smooth and believable changes later.

Follow this step-by-step cheat sheet to do your edits in the right order for optimum quality and safety.

1. Change the photos you want to edit from JPEG files into TIFF files so you won't lose image quality.

2. Make red-eye reductions.

3. Adjust color problems.

4. Adjust brightness and contrast problems.

5. Make creative changes, like cloning or retouching.

6. Save before changing resolution, cropping, or scaling.

7. Make resolution, resampling, and cropping changes.

8. Sharpen the image if necessary.

9. Save as a TIFF for the last time.

10. Save as a JPEG at the correct quality setting.

11. Add type or borders.

12. Delete any previously saved files you no longer want.

Improve
Your Photos

We know that you've read Chapter 3 on how to compose and take good photos, and Chapter 4, which deals with camera options for creating quality images. We also know that once you start shooting pictures you probably won't be reading this book with one hand and shooting with the other. Picture moments happen, and sometimes photographers forget the basics in the excitement of a terrific moment. The inevitable result is photos that, if shot with film, would end up in the circular file.

But since you're using a digital camera, you get a second chance. Just transfer your photos to your computer and fire up a good image-editing program, and you can work miracles. Digital photos are amazingly easy to change, and totally flexible.

In this chapter, you'll apply some image-editing tools and your own imagination and savvy to perfect your pictures. You may start with simply repairing images that are a little too dark or slightly red—but you'll soon find yourself gleefully creating a new photo reality.

Fixing Brightness and Contrast

The most common problem with digital pictures is shots that are too dark or too light. Unlike composition or focus problems that you can see on the LCD screen, you can't always tell if your photo will have good tonal quality (*tone* is the combination of brightness and contrast) until you can see it more clearly. Having the tools and skills to repair these problems will help you salvage many a picture and will earn you the reputation of an accomplished photographer.

Ideally, you should be working with a program that has a Levels tool. But even if you don't, you can still improve the tone of many pictures with brightness and contrast sliders.

Before you try to make any corrections in your image, change your image from color to grayscale. (Some editing software, like iPhoto, has a button to do this quickly. In other software, look for a Mode menu and select grayscale from the list.) Does the picture still look too bright or dark? If so, undo the grayscale setting and continue editing. But you may be surprised to discover that your picture looks perfectly fine in grayscale. If so, changing the image brightness will simply make your image worse.

If you have enough room on your screen, make a duplicate copy of the file you're editing and place it on the screen behind the file you're working on. It helps to compare the two to make sure that your changes are actually improving, not harming, the photo.

Using Brightness and Contrast Sliders

If your imaging software only has brightness and contrast sliders for tonal changes, you'll have to watch your image very carefully as you edit. A small change can have big consequences. Move the brightness slider first, two or three units to the left or right, depending on your image's problem. If you are going for more brightness, watch the brightest important places on the image as you do this. When they start to lose detail, you've gone too far, no matter how dark the rest of the image looks (**Figure 9.1**). The same goes for darkening: As you make an image darker, you should be watching the detail in the shadows.

Figure 9.1 Look at the cake on the left. All the detail in the frosting is disappearing as the brightness increases. If the bright places are insignificant to the image, you might ignore the problem and keep going. But in this case, the cake cutting is the major action in the photo.

It's a rare picture that can be adjusted without moving both sliders a little. Once you have a brightness setting you can live with, work on the contrast. If you've made a big change in the brightness setting, you'll probably have to decrease the contrast a little, or else bright and dark areas will lose more detail.

In any event, you shouldn't be changing these sliders more than 10 units for a normal picture. You'll find that anything more will either wash out the picture or make it look like it was shot in a cave.

Levels tools that work on one color channel at a time can help color balance, but brightness and contrast sliders can't. If you don't have Levels, you'll need to change the image color balance (using a Hue/Saturation tool), not the image brightness.

Using Levels

Sometimes an image is basically well shot, but it looks soft and dim. If you don't see many things that are bright or very dark, the image doesn't have enough contrast. You can verify this in the Levels histogram (**Figure 9.2**).

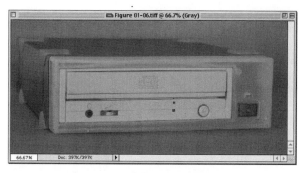
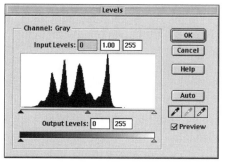

Figure 9.2 This image (left) has all its pixels in the midtones and none in the shadows or highlights, which you can tell from its histogram (right). Although it probably needs brightening, brightening alone (without adjusting the contrast) will eliminate the darker tones, too, resulting in a classic case of poor contrast.

To fix both brightness and contrast, we use the input slider below the histogram picture. As you move the black-and-white arrows into the center, the computer stretches the available pixel shades outward to fill out more of the range from black to white. Since there were no white pixels before, moving the slider brightens the image considerably. That's easy to visualize if you compare the image's new histogram (**Figure 9.3**) with its original one. The range of 255 shades in the new his-

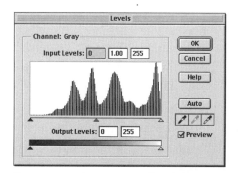

Figure 9.3 After moving the sliders into the middle, the pixels that were bunched up in the center in the histogram in Figure 9.2 have been stretched to fill out the entire tonal range. The result: an image with a good tonal range and contrast.

togram is a little thinner, because you can't invent pixels that aren't there. The original pixels have been altered to stretch the original bunched-up shades across the full range from dark to light.

The middle slider changes the midtones. If your image has lots of contrast already but some areas are too dim, moving the white or black arrows inward will make the image worse. Try moving the midtone slider arrow instead.

Correcting Color Shifts

Red still looks like red when we go from the bright outdoors to a dim room or to an office with fluorescent lights. But the *shade* of red has altered, because the light that hits it no longer has the full spectrum of color. We don't notice, because our brain and eyes adjust and shift all colors equally. But the camera lens doesn't. If the color has shifted because of the type of illumination in a room, the camera will capture the shifted colors. For example, interior incandescent light shifts colors toward the warmer tones of red and yellow. Fluorescents, on the other hand, tend to shift toward the blue and green. People in photographs taken under these different types of light tend to look a little softer and rosier in incandescent, and a little more pale and cadaverous in a typical office photo. The effect of these color shifts can ruin an otherwise well composed and photographed image.

Using Hue/Saturation

It's possible to use the Hue/Saturation slider to fix color shift problems. But how possible depends on the depth of options your image-editing program offers. The most common Hue/Saturation tool works on the entire image and all its channels at once. The problem, of course, is much the same as using the Brightness/Contrast slider: it's all or nothing (**Figure 9.4**).

If the tool in your program is made up of sliders, your best strategy is to move the Hue slider slightly away from the center (toward the green shades if the picture was shot in incandescent light, or toward the red shades if under fluorescent light), then desaturate a little bit.

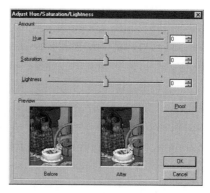

Figure 9.4 In this typical Hue/Saturation dialog box, you will be able to improve your color shift problem, but probably not solve it. You can shift the hue of the color, you can desaturate to make everything less vibrant, or you can lighten the colors to make the color shift less noticeable.

You need to lower the saturation, because moving the Hue slider is a limited fix that can only make the photo less red or green. It can't change a color's brightness, or change its tone to make it a warmer, lighter shade or a deeper, subtler one. It can only correct a red color shift by adding green (rather than the more sensible way: by eliminating red).

Every program's sliders are calibrated a little differently, but you'll probably find acceptable results between –5 and –15 on the Saturation slider. Needless to say, a photograph with an unusually strong color shift, or one with a very slight one, might need slightly more or less than these guidelines.

Photoshop Elements allows you to adjust hue and saturation by color channel, a feature that may not be quite as good as

Photoshop's Curves function, but is a big improvement over all-channel adjustments and a lot easier to figure out than the Curves function. You can choose each of the color channels in turn, and adjust them individually. This is a good way to learn about color shifts, because you can see the results of adding or subtracting color in each channel, rather than overall in the image.

Using Levels

If your program allows you to change levels for each channel individually, a complete color shift repair is within your grasp. Once you master levels for straight tonal values, you can apply that knowledge to color.

What do levels, which change brightness and contrast, have to do with fixing color? Colors in an image are recorded at different levels of brightness, depending on the quality and type of light in which the photo was shot. So if you can change these values in each color channel independently using Levels, you can decrease the brightness of the overly dominant color channel without affecting the channels that are fine. If you can only change brightness and contrast throughout the whole image, you frequently aren't able to optimize an image, because one color channel is dragging the whole image down.

If your image looks good in grayscale but not in color, than one of the three color channels (red, green, or blue) is causing your problem. You need to figure out which one it is. Open the Levels dialog box and examine all three channels. These three histograms were taken from an image shot indoors, with a strong, waxy-yellow cast to it. There's a cake with white frosting in the foreground, but the frosting looks creamy yellow, not pure white the way it should be.

One of the things you look for in a histogram is a place where pixels are either very heavily distributed, or nonexistent. Those places are clues to what may be missing or skewed in an image. In this example, the red channel has its ups and downs, but there is red throughout the image (**Figure 9.5**). Green is less evenly distributed, but is certainly present in both the brightest and darkest regions.

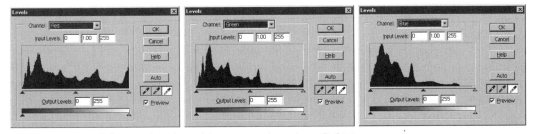

Figure 9.5 From left to right, these histograms show how light is distributed in each channel (red, green, and blue) of the image.

But the blue channel is skewed. Although there is plenty of blue at one end, at the other end there's practically no blue at all. We'd like more blue at the bright end on the right so

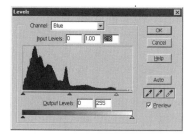

that the mix of colors in the white cake will go from red/green (which is how the computer makes yellow) to a nice neutral white. When we move the white point on the histogram to the left, the frosting whitens, and all the other colors brighten up as well. Mission accomplished.

Altering and Editing Images

All of the changes we've talked about so far involve things that you might have been able to correct in your camera settings before even taking the shot or, if using a traditional camera, in the darkroom. But the most fun aspects of editing digital photos are the things you could never do with a traditional setup: the changes that play games with reality.

You definitely need image-editing tools to make the changes in this section: selection tools, masking, a cloning tool, a dodge-and-burn tool, and layers. Bear in mind that the following are examples. Unlike photographic changes, image retouching is different for every image you retouch. The suggestions are general; you'll have to adapt them to the program you use and each picture you take.

Making People Look Better

Of all the things you might edit in your photos, fixing people's faces can be the most satisfying. If there's anything that people hate to see, it's their blemishes, wrinkles, and shadows. Remove them well, and everyone will ask for reprints. Do it not so well, and your spouse will hide your camera before you leave the house.

Let's start with wrinkles. Here's a typical photo from a get-together—everyone is in a fine mood and feeling no pain (**Figure 9.6**). But the woman will not be smiling so broadly when she sees that wrinkle on her forehead in sharp relief. This is a job for the cloning tool.

As with most editing projects, you'll want to zoom up to make delicate changes. When you do, pay attention to the color and lighting of the area you want to fix. The reason the wrinkle is so obvious is that it's fairly deep, and the area right next to it is brightly reflecting the camera flash. Your mission is to clone from an area nearby so you can lighten the wrinkle and darken the highlight that puts it in sharp relief.

We'll begin by darkening the highlight. Choose a soft brush that is not much wider than the area you need to repair. Then Alt or Option-click with your cloning tool (or whatever key and mouse combination that picks up a sample for your cloning tool) on a portion of the image that looks like it has the right amount of

Figure 9.6 No one wants to see their wrinkles highlighted for the world to see.

darkness to be the skin color that would have been there had there been no wrinkle. We've selected a place on the forehead close to the wrinkle, but to the side of its shadow.

If your cloning tool doesn't have blend options or alignment capabilities, you should slowly run your brush down a few pixels of the wrinkle and highlight, then stop and sample from the forehead area again before moving a little further down. Continual sampling prevents the cloning tool from using the original forehead area as a

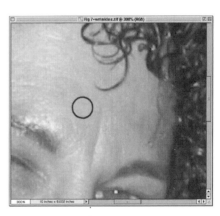

starting point and moving into a lower part of the forehead for its sample. This is tedious, but it's the only way to make sure that you don't move into a darker or lighter area.

If your cloning tool offers a Continuous or Aligned option, deselect it so that you can keep drawing samples from the exact place on the face that you need. Choose Darken from the blend options, then position your cloning tool over the highlight. The nifty thing about Darken is that it only changes pixels that are lighter than the area you sampled, so it won't touch the wrinkle itself; and it doesn't copy the texture or color of the sample area, so you won't have an obvious patch where you cloned.

Don't try to fix the area in one stroke (**Figure 9.7**). Work in batches until you're done, moving down the highlight area to guarantee that you've continued to sample from the exact area (with the exact lighting) you need.

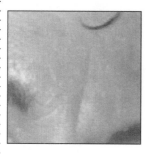

Figure 9.7 The highlight on the wrinkle has been eliminated to halfway down the wrinkle. Notice how much less obvious it is, even though you haven't retouched the wrinkle itself.

If you look at the picture now, without the highlight the wrinkle looks shallower—even though we haven't changed the wrinkle itself. The woman in the picture still looks the way people know her, but just a little better (**Figure 9.8**).

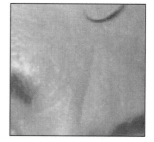

Figure 9.8 The highlight is now completely gone, and with it goes the emphasis on the wrinkle.

If you want to get rid of the wrinkle as well, you'll work the same way as before, but you'll choose Lighten rather than Darken, and you'll select a slightly lighter area of the forehead for the correction. You'll also want to change the transparency setting of the cloning tool as you go, so the area where the wrinkle used to be brightens slightly as you move down and to the left. Graduating the brightness will help the area blend into the highlight by the bridge of the nose (**Figure 9.9**).

Select a bright place on your picture, like a tooth highlight, and set Lighten to 50% to do a terrific job of brightening teeth.

Now, how vain is your subject? Ours has shadows under the eyes she'd want corrected as well (too many late nights, no

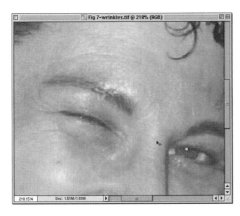

Figure 9.9 We make the area that used to display the wrinkle a little lighter at the very bottom, so it will blend in better with the highlight at the bridge of the nose.

doubt). You could use the same cloning process to correct them, but you'd have to carefully select different sample areas for each subtle change. That's pretty tedious. Instead, choose the Dodge tool (**Figure 9.10**). If you use it at full force, the Dodge tool will wreck your picture. But if you carefully choose the tonal range you want to affect (in our case, Midtones) and if you keep the percentage of change down low enough (we've started low at 20 percent), Dodge will work wonders.

Figure 9.10 This Dodge tool is set to a 9-pixel-wide, soft-edged brush, and will only lighten midtone areas that it touches. Its Exposure setting determines how much impact it will have on an area with each stroke.

The result: the woman looks 10 years younger, and a lot more rested. Don't be surprised if everyone asks for the same treatment (**Figure 9.11**).

Figure 9.11 You can remove wrinkles and even out skin tone without plastic surgery or Botox injections.

When using the Dodge and Burn tools, avoid moving back and forth over the same area. Every time you go over the same pixels, the effect is multiplied.

Cloning Hints

Bad results happen even with a professional cloning tool if you are new to the technique. Although each image has its own needs, here are some general hints for successful cloning:

- If you're editing out an object, choose your sample (the area you're copying from) as close to the target (the area you're cloning to) as you can.

- Watch changes in light and shadow. If your sample moves from dark to light but your target is in full light, your clone will look like a patch.

- Pay attention to texture—it's almost as important as light and shadow. Things that are farther away will be softer and less textured than things that are made of the same material but seen up close.

- Avoid a hard-edged brush for touch-ups. If you make a mistake, it will be more obvious.

- Start with a small-diameter brush. Most beginners start with big brushes to make the work move faster, but good cloning takes time and patience.

- Work over small areas and reselect a sample area frequently to avoid using part of the target area as the sample as you move across the image.

- Remember that the real world isn't perfect, and an exact clone will stand out like a sore thumb. If you want natural-looking results, slightly vary your sample sources as you paint.

- Experiment! Although time-consuming at the beginning, cloning offers great image-editing power. Play with different tool settings and techniques, and have fun with your ideas.

Erasing Large Objects

Erasing large objects from an image can be tedious, but there are some shortcuts. Generally, the more material you have to draw from, the easier changes will be. You must have enough bits and pieces of similar material that you can seamlessly fix and replace, since big objects often call for cut, paste, and layer tools.

Look for portions of the image that could be pasted directly into the missing area without looking strange. It would take a pretty remarkable cloning job to get the precision of a machined curve as you clone, so you need a different editing strategy and some different image-editing tools. Man-made objects like cars, bottles, and plates are symmetrical. You can often copy a portion of a symmetrically shaped object, flip it, and graft it to the other side of the object (**Figure 9.12**). To eliminate the unwanted white area in the lower right of the image, we first select the left side of the plate and table. Then we make a new layer, and copy and paste the selected area into it. Once we have the layer in place, we flip it horizontally, so the left half is now in the correct direction and ready to be grafted into place in the lower right of the image. Don't be surprised if you have to rotate your mirrored area slightly to get the edges to line up. It's difficult to shoot a picture precisely square on, and much easier to make adjustments on the computer.

Figure 9.12 In this example, we have a lovely dinner shot, but there's an unexpected white object in the lower right. So we cut and paste a portion from the left side of the image, flip it, and graft it onto the lower-right corner to, in effect, eliminate the unwanted object.

Photoshop Elements has a tool called Layer via Copy that handles the work of cutting, pasting, and creating the layer for you.

Layer...	⇧⌘N
Layer From Background	
Layer via Copy	⌘J
Layer via Cut	⇧⌘J

Now erase any of the material you mirrored from the left side that you don't really need. The lighting from the left isn't exactly a perfect match for the right side—and besides, you want to preserve as much of what the camera actually saw as possible. Decrease the transparency of the top layer, so the bottom area shows through while you cut away the excess from the copied section on the top layer (**Figure 9.13**).

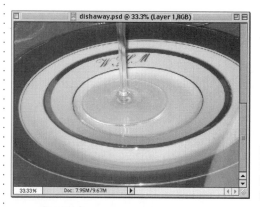

Figure 9.13 You can see both layers while you trim extra parts of the copied portion.

Figure 9.14 We've balanced the lighting so that the copied piece blends in seamlessly to complete the still life.

Probably one side of the object was lighter than the other. If you take the extra time to fix the lighting, you'll be happier with the result. If there's a big difference, you may have a lot of work ahead of you. It will be easier to use the Burn tool to darken one side successfully than to lighten the mirror image. The Dodge tool is good at slightly lightening areas that are too dark (**Figure 9.14**).

Creating a Mask

A photo mask, like a mask you wear, covers and protects an area of a photo. But unlike a face mask, it (usually) protects the area you *haven't* selected, so you can make changes to the part that you have (see Chapter 8). Masks are also used to separate a portion of an image from its background, so you can merge part of an image with a completely different second image.

To create a mask, you first define an area of the image with your selection tools. The quality of your mask will be better if you have a wide range of tool options. (See Chapter 8 for more on selection tools.) Not all photo software allows you to mask a portion of an image, although most image-editing software does. If your software includes the option of putting pieces of images on separate layers, it probably also has masking. Look at your software's documentation to find out where the masking tool is, and how to apply it.

Some things are easy to mask, like objects with clearly defined or straight edges. Other things are so difficult to mask that either you'll have to accept a less-than-perfect result or you should reconsider the project. Are you masking around curly hair or fur, or straight hair that's blowing in the wind? Their imprecise edges make these kinds of fuzzy objects hard to mask, because they have tiny bits of color that are distinctly visible but next to impossible to select without special tools. **Figure 9.15** shows a cat's fur and whiskers. We've used the magic wand to select the black background, in order to replace it with another one. But there are bits and pieces of black showing behind the cat's fur, and there's no easy way to add those pieces to the selection. If we don't add them, however, we'll have a black halo behind the cat no matter what background we try to put in place of the original.

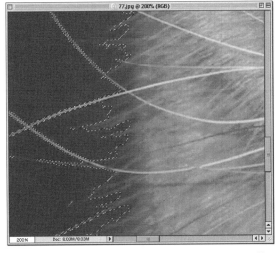

Figure 9.15 The magic wand just can't select all the bits and pieces of black showing behind the cat's fur. We need more sophisticated selection tools than our program provides.

Masking is also easier if the background is significantly lighter or darker than the foreground object you want to mask. If the image background doesn't have a lot of contrast with the foreground, you could have a rough time separating the two.

If you're trying to combine two images, you'll get better results if the lighting in both pictures is similar. If you have a picture with light coming from the front, for example, you can't merge it with a picture of the setting sun. The lighting is so different that the image will look surreal (**Figure 9.16**). (Of course, if you want surreal, that's the best way to do it!)

Figure 9.16 In this example, we have two originals: a shot of a house on an overcast day (top left), and a shot on a bright, sunny day (top right). When we merge the roof and dormer of the bright shot onto the overcast one (left), the strong contrast and shadows on the top part of the house look wrong with the rest of the house.

Print Your Images

10

We love the instant gratification of seeing pictures onscreen, but there's still nothing like having a color print. Although fashionable technocrats may carry their laptops everywhere to show off their pictures digitally, most people pass around snapshots—at the office, at the Thanksgiving table, at a play date. Fortunately, it's just as easy to make prints from your digital images as from traditional film. Easier, actually, since you don't even have to leave your house to drop off and pick up prints. In this chapter, we cover your printing options, from using your own printer to the many ways you can pass the work on to professionals.

Why Print at Home?

Admittedly, professional services are a real time- and hassle-saver. Besides, unless you were a serious photo hobbyist (or professional), you never processed your pictures by yourself with a regular camera. Why bother with it now?

Because you can. Film processing is messy, smelly, and even potentially bad for you. Setting up a darkroom is expensive and requires a dedicated room. But setting up for digital printing merely requires plugging one USB cable into your computer and installing a printer driver. The printer takes up little space, and the only way it can harm you is if you drop one on your toe.

A

B

C

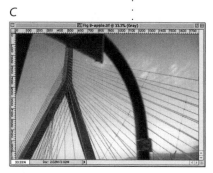

Figure 10.1 (A) the original print, with the base of the bridge lit and the sky extending above; (B) our 4 x 6-inch Snapfish print; (C) our print from Apple. Apple's technician sharpened and set a white point for this picture, which is good for photos of people, but not necessarily right for other types of shots.

Because you want it now. At home, you shoot, you print. At the photo service, you shoot, you upload (or drop off), then you wait. Waiting actually feels worse for digital prints, because you've already seen them onscreen and know how good they are. And waiting is all the more frustrating because you know you have a relatively easy alternative if you want to use it.

Because you won't get your whole print otherwise. Digital cameras take pictures at a different aspect ratio than photo services print them. So if you shoot a 2048 x 1536-pixel photo, you've shot a 4.5 x 6-inch snapshot. But when you get that picture back from a professional developer, they've run it through a cookie cutter to make it 4 x 6 inches, slicing off some of your picture in the process. You lose bits and pieces in other sizes as well. Of course, unless you cut the picture down yourself first, you can't control what the photo service will trim. In some pictures that's not so serious. But in others, it matters.

Because you may not get what you shot otherwise. As you can see in **Figure 10.1**, we sent the same print to two different services: Snapfish and Apple. Both use Kodak developing services. Snapfish kept the brightness and value about right, but the picture was a little too fuzzy and was cropped smaller than 4 inches. Apple produced a crisp and perfect 4 x 6 but brightened the photo to look like afternoon, not dusk. If you printed the picture yourself on an inkjet, you could adjust the output to look exactly the way you remembered the scene.

Inkjet Printers and Cartridges

To print at home, you need a photo-quality color printer. Inkjet printers are your best choice if you want to use one printer for both photos and text.

If you're willing to make a bigger investment, there are printers that produce prints of the quality and durability of traditional photographic prints.

Dye-sublimation printers used to be too expensive for anyone but professionals, but consumer models now sell for less than $500. Dye-sub printers employ a sheet of dye-imbued film that transfers color to special paper via a heating element. The results are impressive—but so is the cost of materials. The paper and dye for a single print can run as high as a dollar, compared with the pennies you'll spend for an inkjet print. Dye subs also take longer to print, and the less expensive models print at only one size: 3 x 5 inches.

Buying Considerations

You can buy a multipurpose inkjet printer for under $100. A basic photo inkjet will cost closer to $150. In most cases, the technology of a $150 photo printer won't be much different than one that costs $500. The differences? More expensive printers usually process more information, which also tends to make them slower. They're also larger, enabling you to print your own blowups. And they often have larger-capacity inkjet cartridges.

Some printers have built-in card readers, so you can insert your storage card right into the printer and either upload the pictures to the computer or print directly. Unless the printer has a way to view the pictures on the storage card (some do), the direct print option may not be as useful as reviewing your work on the computer and then deciding which shots you actually want to print.

Make sure that the printer you choose has the software to make it work with your computer. The best printer is of little value of you can't use it. For example, many older inkjet printers that you might find on eBay won't work with Mac OS X.

Unless dye subs become truly inexpensive commodities, most people will continue to buy inkjet printers for their photos. To get a print good enough to rival a traditional film print, your printer will need to produce at a high resolution: 2400 x 1200 dots per inch (dpi) or better. But inkjet printers in that range have become very affordable.

General-Purpose vs. Photo

One of the big misconceptions about inkjet printers is that if you purchase a printer that promises photo quality, you've got the right printer for photos. In fact, there are two different types of color inkjet printers: general purpose and photo. Your choice can make all the difference in the quality and durability of your photo prints.

General-purpose printers are used for a variety of home and business purposes, with photo printing part of the mix. *Photo printers* use specially formulated inks and paper that are optimized for photographic images. Although you can frequently use the same paper in both types, and a photo printed at the same resolution on both can look almost the same, they are really very different products. General-purpose inkjets, like

Epson's Stylus, series are cheap and fast. Because they're seen as small-business printers, they're optimized for text rather than image, and they print reasonably well on plain laser paper. The glossy paper made for them is thin and cheaper than that used by photo printers. Because general-purpose inkjets aren't optimized for photos, you're more likely to see color shifts and dither (see "What Is Dither?").

Photo printers not only will give you better quality pictures, but those pictures will last longer. Many photo printers use special inks and papers to make them more resistant to moisture and fading. (Spill liquid on a typical inkjet print just once, and you'll know why water resistance is a good idea!) Those special inks are one of the reasons that photo printers are a little more expensive to own and run. And because a photo print needs lots of ink, some photo printers run through cartridges a little faster than all-purpose printers. They are often slower as well, which can be frustrating if you want your print and you want it now.

 If you've already bought a general-purpose printer, check out third-party makers of inks and paper. Some enterprising companies are making waterproof paper and inks for non–photo printers.

Despite these limitations, you should unquestionably buy a photo printer if most of your printing will be for digital photos. You can still print lower-quality prints for other purposes, but you will be less likely to find yourself reprinting a photo that's turning blue with age.

If you don't want to buy a printer, buy a camera that's a printer as well. Just like the old Polaroid cameras, the Olympus C-211 does it all. It's too large for extreme sport trips, but for most purposes it's a good way to get immediate gratification.

What Is Dither?

Dither is a good thing, as long as you can't see it. It is a way of using patterns to lay down printer inks. A good dither pattern will trick the eye into seeing one merged color instead of four or six individual ones—although you'll still detect the individual dots of color if you look very closely on a low-resolution print, or under a magnifying glass with a high-resolution one (see **Figure 10.2**).

Dithering is used for all color printing on paper—if you look closely you can see it in color photos in newspapers and comic books.

Figure 10.2 Both of these swatches are blown up to 400 percent. The printout on the left is from an inkjet printer at low resolution, making it easier to see that the printer lays down dots, rather than continuous color like with a paintbrush. The printout on the right has a higher resolution that makes it harder to perceive the dots.

Types of Cartridges

Individual cartridges aren't very expensive, but their cost can add up faster than you anticipate if you fail to read the fine print. Look carefully at the number of prints the manufacturer says you'll be able to make per cartridge. Hidden away on a data sheet is the degree of *coverage* (the percentage of the blank page that is actually covered with ink) that determines the number of prints you can expect. Many manufacturers rate their cartridges based on a coverage of 15 percent. But if you'll be using the printer for photography, your coverage will be much higher—perhaps as high as 100 percent if you're printing an 8 x 10 print on 8.5 x 11-inch paper. Translation: You'll be getting far fewer prints per cartridge, and you'll be changing those cartridges frequently.

Because you'll be burning through cartridges furiously, you'll want to look at the type of cartridge your printer uses. Manufacturers can choose between two cartridge configurations. They can make a printer with two cartridges: one for black and one for the other three colors (cyan, magenta, and yellow), or they can create individual cartridges for each color.

It's more convenient—and cost-effective—for the manufacturer to make only two cartridges. Fewer cartridges are more convenient for you, the consumer, as well. You don't have to pay attention to which ink of a set is going bad, and you don't have to constantly keep an inventory of how many cartridges of each color you have. On the other hand, this tricolor concept wastes ink, because you're unlikely to use all three colors equally fast. You'll end up throwing out cartridges that still have plenty of ink because a single color has run dry. And because tricolor cartridges also tend to contain very little ink per color well, you'll be changing (and discarding) cartridges more frequently—an environmental concern.

Unfortunately, most of Epson's inexpensive color printers use this three-plus-one model, and Epson, as of this writing, is the largest seller of photo inkjet printers. We hope that the release of the Epson C80 Stylus printer indicates that Epson has revisited its color cartridge decisions. This new printer model follows the HP photo printer lead in offering four high-capacity ink cartridges but also offers true photo quality and longevity in an all-purpose printer.

On the other hand, when it comes to the number of colors in the printer, more is always better. If your printer has six ink colors (Epson adds light cyan and light magenta to the usual four in some of its photo printers), you'll see better detail with smoother shading between color changes. Skin tones in particular will be more realistic and delicate. Your prints will look as good (or even better) than an equivalent image printed by a professional service. The big drawback to six-color printers is, of course, price. Not only are they more expensive to buy, but each picture will be more expensive to print. Right now, six-color printers are used more by professional graphic designers and photographers who need very high quality output.

Maintaining Your Printer

Part of printing successfully is keeping your printer in good condition. If your print cartridge nozzles clog, you'll get prints with ugly lines through them at regular intervals. It's true that cleaning these nozzles uses up inks more quickly, but not cleaning them also uses up ink, and wastes time besides. Most printers have a cleaning utility to help you maintain good quality (**Figure 10.3**). You might also want to invest in a print-head cleaning kit if your print heads are so blocked that your software utility can't clean them.

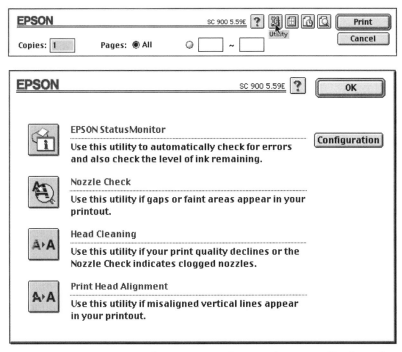

Figure 10.3 On a Macintosh, you access Epson's cleaning utility from the little Tools icon in the upper-right corner of its Print dialog box (top). The utility lets you view how much ink you have left in your cartridges, calibrate your print head, and clean the color print heads (bottom).

You can do some simple things to help maintain print quality. If you don't use your printer frequently, turn it off when it's not in use. Many printers seal off the inks when you turn the printer off, which makes the inks last longer and decreases print-head clogging. Even better, use the printer frequently. Frequent use is probably the best thing you can do to keep your print quality up to par.

If you have a photo printer, avoid using regular copier or uncoated laser paper in it. This type of paper is rougher than photo paper and can leave a residue inside the printer. Lightly vacuuming, or even blowing out the residue with compressed air, can also help.

If your printer freezes up noisily, using a lubricating oil (like WD-40) on the chrome strip the print head rides on might save you a trip to the repair shop. Use a clean cloth, and apply it sparingly to avoid getting oil inside the rest of the printer.

Choosing Your Paper

As mentioned above, for photo prints you should avoid plain copier paper, stationery, or other nonphoto paper. And if you use paper that was specifically created for your inkjet, you'll get better results than if you use generic inkjet paper, or paper that was formulated for a different brand of inkjet. The wrong paper can make colors look dull and muddy because the inks bleed into each other instead of remaining in their dither pattern. Sometimes text will look OK when printed on a different brand of paper—say, HP paper on an Epson printer. But the print may not last as long, or it may begin to turn unexpected colors as it ages. Sticking to your own printer's paper shouldn't cramp your style too much. You'll still have a variety of papers to experiment with.

Paper Types

Paper types can be confusing if you don't know the terminology. Essentially, you need to consider two things when buying paper: weight and finish.

Paper is measured by how much a ream (500 sheets) of a given paper type weighs. The larger the number, the heavier the sheets of paper are. For example, copier paper is very thin and usually weighs 20 pounds. Inexpensive inkjet paper is between 20 and 22 pounds. Good laser paper and stationery sheets are usually 24 pounds. Needless to say, the heavier the paper, the more the paper costs.

Photo paper needs to be thicker than standard office or inkjet paper. In most office printing, large areas of the paper are left blank, or are printed only with type. But to print a photo, you cover the entire sheet with ink, so you need a paper that won't bend and buckle like a wet newspaper.

Even within photo papers, there are differences in weight. For example, Epson's Photo Paper is 52 pounds, and their Premium Glossy Photo Paper is 68 pounds (**Figure 10.4**). Both will give you a glossy, photo-quality print, but the lighter weight feels flimsier than the type of paper professional photo services print on.

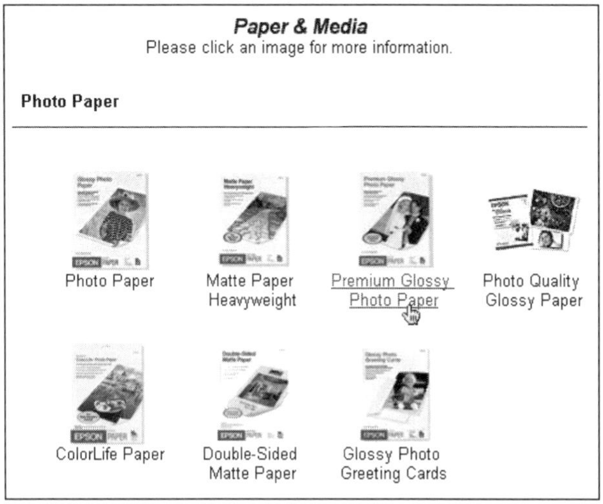

You would think that a heavier paper is also a thicker paper, and most of the time you'd be right. But sometimes a lighter paper can be thicker than a heavier one, much as an angel food cake will rise higher than a pecan pie but still not represent as much bulk.

Figure 10.4 You may have to dig a little through the manufacturer's Web site, but if you want to know the weight of a paper before you buy it, look for the detailed specs in the manufacturer's supplies section.

That's why many nonglossy papers called "heavyweight" may actually only be 44-pound paper but will feel more substantial than a glossy sheet of the same poundage.

Thicker is not always better for you. Some printers aren't designed to print on very heavy paper. They have problems picking it up and keeping it straight, resulting in prints that are actually worse than they would be on thinner paper.

The other important consideration—more an issue of aesthetics than quality—is the paper finish. Like house paint, paper finishes ranges from matte (which is a flat, nonreflective but smooth finish), to satin (which is coated but not very shiny) to high gloss (which can be so shiny that is brightly reflects direct light). There are a variety of finishes in between with rather imprecise names: soft gloss, semigloss, or just plain gloss. Your choice is a matter of taste, of course, but some finishes lend themselves better to different types of usage. If you plan to display a photo in bright light, you should probably steer away from a high-gloss paper, because people looking at it will see the reflections better than they will the photo.

Of course, before you buy a paper, check to see that it's one your printer manufacturer recommends (**Figure 10.5**). If you've bought a photo printer because its prints are more durable and less likely to fade, you negate that virtue by buying a paper that is not for-mulated for long life, even if the initial results seem fine.

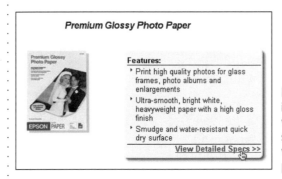

Figure 10.5 Every inkjet manufacturer will have detailed specs on its Web site with recommended paper choices.

Keep your paper in its package until you use it, and pay attention to which direction (face up or down) your printer needs the printing surface to be. Your prints may success-fully print on both sides of matte paper, but they will proba-bly smear terribly on the back of glossy, messing up the inside of your printer in the process.

Special Papers

Your printer manufacturer also offers papers for special types of projects. There are transfer papers that let you transfer your photos and type to make one-of-a-kind T-shirts, transparency papers that let you use your photos in a presentation, and papers with a sticky backing that let you turn your prints into labels or personal stickers.

Making Your Inkjet Photos Last Forever

OK, nothing lasts forever, not even traditional photographs. Have you ever walked by a real estate office and seen all the photos of houses? You can see which ones have been on the market too long by the amount of fade in the color. But digital prints used to be worse. People used to complain bitterly about how quickly the prints faded compared with traditional photos. Some prints still do, because many printer inks are really not formulated for longevity. But, with few exceptions, if you purchase a photo printer today and follow some basic guidelines, your prints can easily last as long as a Kodak print from your local drugstore or online service.

- Use the right paper and inks. Your printer can print with a range of inks and media, but not all will last as long as others. Read your printer documentation's paper and ink recommendations carefully.

- Give prints time to dry. Matte papers dry faster than glossy paper, but all photo prints need a little time to "set." Don't stack your prints immediately after you print them.

- Keep prints out of direct sunlight. Light is the enemy of all photo prints, whether traditional or digital.

- Frame your prints properly if you want to display them. A print under glass will last, even in daylight, considerably longer than one left in the open air. Some people recommend special UV (ultraviolet) glass, but from our experience that isn't necessary except for prints made from multipurpose inkjet printers, or prints that will have a direct incandescent spotlight on them.

- Watch out for "magnetic" photo albums. The stuff that makes the plastic stick to the page can react with your inkjet prints, with horrid results.

- Stay away from heat and moisture. Extreme heat can cause chemical changes in photo paper and inks. And many inkjets use a water-based formulation. The combination will make prints stick together, bleed color, and otherwise ruin some perfect photo moments.

In addition, some companies create papers for specialized needs. Such papers are usually a safe exception to the "use the manufacturer's recommended paper" rule. Professional digital photographers use these specialty papers all the time. They offer special finishes and levels of brightness for just about any project you can imagine. Some will give your photo the feeling of a painting—nice if you're experimenting with the watercolor or other filters in your image- or photo-editing program (**Figure 10.6**).

Figure 10.6 This watercolor image is perfect for printing on an art paper.

Setting Up Your Image

The most important part of setting up your image is making sure that you're printing at the right print resolution and print size. Of course, we hope that you shot your picture at the right resolution for the print dimensions you want (see "Print Sizes and Print Resolution").

You can print from several file formats successfully, although we recommend using TIFF if you plan to scale your picture up or down just before you print. The JPEG format (which is what your camera produces unless you set it to something else) is fine if you print at 100 percent after resampling. (See "Changing Resolution and Size," in Chapter 8 to learn about resampling and changing resolution and print settings.)

Printing Several Images on One Page

The default for printing is one page of paper, one print. But there's no reason to waste all that empty space. You can frequently fit more than one snapshot on a standard letter-size page.

Print Sizes and Print Resolution

Although you can print your photos at any resolution, your results will be lower quality than a traditional photo print if your resolution is too low for the size you want to print at. What's too low? Everyone's tolerance for jagged edges is slightly different, and some types of pictures (like ones with high contrast) require better resolution than others. For most people, 100 pixels per inch (ppi) is the threshold between acceptable and not. Most people consider 150 ppi acceptable for snapshots. If you want prints that look professional, you'll need a minimum resolution of 250 ppi, although we recommend 300 ppi for best results.

How does the print resolution correspond to your camera resolutions? This chart helps you estimate what will work for you. The middle columns show camera resolution.

Desired print size (inches)	Acceptable	Preferred	Megapixel level needed for preferred resolution
2.5 x 3.5 (wallet size)	640 x 480	1024 x 768	any digital camera
3.5 x 5 (snapshot)	1024 x 768	1600 x 1200	1 megapixel
4 x 6 (large snapshot)	1024 x 768	1712 x 1200	2 megapixels
5 x 7	1152 x 864	2048 x 1536	3.2 megapixels
8 x 10	1600 x 1200	2272 x1 704*	4.1 megapixels*
11 x 14	1712 x 1200		

*4.1 megapixels is currently the highest resolution camera you can buy before moving to extremely high-end professional options.

You'll find that photo services tend to round down on acceptable resolutions. For example, every photo service will tell you that you can make good 5 x 7-inch prints from a 1600 x 1200-pixel shot. But if you compare the same picture from the same service, printed at 4 x 6 and 5 x 7, you'll probably notice that the larger print is a little less crisp and color-true. Good, yes. Great, no.

If you want to print two or more copies of the same picture on a page, you may find that your photo software has a function to set up multiple copies automatically. For example, Photoshop Elements has a Picture Package function that lets you choose just about any configuration of multiples; the software figures out how to make it work on the page size you've chosen (**Figure 10.7**) Once you've printed the sheets, all you have to do is cut the paper in half. But if you plan to print several 4 x 6 snapshots, check the specialty papers your printer manufacturer offers. Chances are there's a perforated paper for printing two snapshots on the same sheet.

Figure 10.7 Elements' Picture Package option doesn't change the original picture. It creates a new file with multiples of the original picture, scaled and positioned to fit on the page. In this case, Cyndi has chosen to fill the page with wallet-size pictures of her niece.

Printing different photos on the same sheet of photo paper (so you can fit two or more prints on the same page) takes a little more work, but it's not too difficult. HP photo printers come with imaging software that has a function for printing more than one photo on a page.

If you aren't using an HP printer, you still have many ways to save paper. Look for programs that have custom layout templates. Many of them will have a printing template as part of the mix. For example, Windows shareware programs, among them PrintSix (www.sixdigitalphotos.com) and PrintStation (www.picmeta.com), let you print multiple different photos on the same page. Another good option is PhotoPrinter from Arc-Soft (the same people who created the nifty PhotoImpression image editing software). For Mac OS X, check out Portraits & Prints Template Maker™ (www.econtechnologies.com). It's an inexpensive program that allows you to create custom templates for any photo size or any number of photos per page.

If you don't have software with a function that does the work for you, you can still do it yourself. In any program, open up the files you want to print and check their document print size to make sure they're already set to the size and resolution you need. Create a new document the size of the paper you want to print on. Then just copy and paste the pictures into the new document (**Figure 10.8**). When you have them all in place, print the new document.

Figure 10.8 In Photoshop Elements, you can use the Move tool to drag an open picture and duplicate it in a new document. We've done that with two pictures, aligning them against a guide on the left to make it easier to cut them apart when we're done.

Having Professionals Do It

We like to print some photos ourselves, particularly after a serious photo collage session or when we've just shot pictures at a party and want to give everyone a souvenir to take home. But if you're as serious a photo taker as we think you are, you'll probably shoot dozens of pictures at a time, particularly on vacation. When you've got 60 shots to print, chances are sitting in front of a computer for a few hours after you get home is going to feel like a chore. Fortunately, there are lots of companies practically jumping up and down for the opportunity to do all that printing for you.

Local Printing Services

In an effort to attract your photo-printing dollars and to compete with online services, companies have come up with creative ways to print your digital photos. Many camera shops that do film processing can accept your digital storage media, too. But be careful to delete any pictures you don't want from your storage card before handing it over to a local service. Their standard policy to is to print everything on the card, whether you wanted it printed or not. And remember, you can't edit a photo first if you hand the card directly to a service bureau.

On the other hand, these companies may offer choices that many online services don't, like printing on matte paper or same-day or rush service. In some areas, you can find self-service digital printing kiosks in camera stores or even chain stores like Wal-Mart. You can instantly make basic image corrections like red-eye reduction, then print one or many copies of an image right from your storage card. Prices tend to be higher than with online services, but if you're on the road and want a quick print or two, this is a great way to go (**Figure 10.9**).

Figure 9.9 Photo-printing kiosks are cropping up all over the United States as more and more people use digital cameras and want instant results.

Online Photo Printing Services

All of the action in digital photo developing is happening online. There are dozens of services where you can upload your digital photos and order prints to be delivered directly to you.

All online services are not the same, although most have similar elements. Once you've uploaded pictures to a service, you can count on being able to store them at the service, post them in an album or Web page, and get standard 4 x 6 prints. Some services also offer special services: They give tips on taking good pictures, offer photo-editing options, provide templates for projects, or offer customized photo albums (**Figure 10.10**).

Figure 10.10 Ofoto is one of many companies that let you put your pictures onto greeting cards for special occasions.

On the downside, there were once hundreds of sites for photo printing and sharing. Most of them are now out of business. Of those that remain, some are more solvent than others, and thus more likely to be around next week when you tell your friends about your new photo Web site. Ofoto (www.ofoto.com) is owned by Kodak, so you can be pretty sure it'll be a longer term survivor. iPhoto, of course, is just as stable as its owner, Apple Computer (www.apple.com), which currently looks very stable indeed. Snapfish (www.snapfish.com) is also owned by a larger, professional photo company, and is one of the most popular printing services on the Internet because of its pricing and quality.

Speaking of quality—that varies as well. iPhoto and Snapfish get particularly high marks from most users, but they aren't the only ones. Plenty of sites use the same photo-finishing technology as those two, and as long as a company's technicians are competent, you should get pictures that meet your needs.

Setting up an account is usually easy. In most cases, all you need to do is supply an email address, a password, and your full name and address (for mailing your prints back to you).

Most photo services only recognize JPEGs. If you're shooting in RAW format, or editing in TIFF, don't forget to turn your pictures into JPEGs before you send them to the online service.

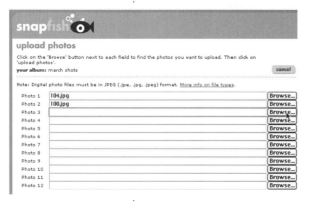

Uploading and Ordering Photos

All well-run photo services have programs that let you browse your computer's hard drive for the photos you want to upload. Usually they ask you to create a named destination for your upload, which helps you organize your files later. Pay attention as you upload: Most sites don't check to see if you've uploaded the same picture twice. And don't overburden your upload with too many photos the first time you send pictures to a site. Send one typical photo first to see how long the process takes with your connection and their server. We particularly like sites like Snapfish that give you a way to cancel an upload, or interrupt it if it's taking too long, and that tell you when the upload is finished (**Figure 10.11**).

If you have a lot of photos to send, consider uploading early in the morning, and on weekdays. Traffic can get pretty heavy on Saturday and Sunday afternoons.

Just as it's a little more expensive to purchase the basics for a digital camera, it's a little more expensive to get professional prints from them as well. You can bring a roll of 24 exposures to the local drug store and pay around $7 to $10 for the privilege. That's between 30 and 40 cents a print, and you usually get doubles of each photo at no extra charge. The lowest prices for digital prints can be twice that amount, and you pay extra for each double print (though prices are sure to drop as volume rises). Plus, you'll be charged shipping costs. To avoid being disappointed, be sure to check the resolution of your prints against the recommendations in "Print Sizes and Resolution," above, before you upload.

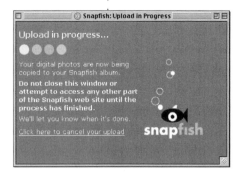

Figure 10.11 Snapfish lets you cancel an upload at any point in the process.

You might also have to cultivate some patience in return for convenience. You won't get your prints the same day or even overnight, the way you can from a fast print or drugstore service. In fact, you could wait a week before the prints arrive.

Prints from iPhoto (Mac OS X Only)

One of the many delightful things about iPhoto is that it isn't exactly an online service. Once your account is set up, the decision and ordering process takes place offline. After Cyndi experienced mammoth delays when she tried to place orders at Microsoft's photo site (photos.msn.com) and her shopping cart at Snapfish froze in the middle of the authorization process (the scariest time for a freeze, because you don't know whether or not the order has been processed), she finds being able to do everything offline—except the actual upload—a blessing.

Sensibly, iPhoto sees all aspects of moving photos out of your computer and into the world as similar tasks. You access all of these options through the Share button (**Figure 10.12**), whether you are viewing the entire photo library or only an album—

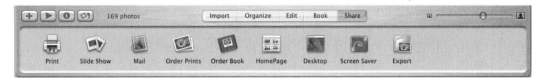

Figure 10.12 Click the Share button, and your sharing options, including ways to print, appear as icons below. If you want to order prints directly from iPhoto, you click the Order Prints icon. The program leads you through the process from that point.

although if you have an album open when you select Share, only the photos in that album will be available for printing.

iPhoto uses Kodak's print service, as do many other photo service providers like AOL and Ofoto. Prices for standard 4 x 6 prints through iPhoto are very reasonable compared to other online options, although their prices for other sizes are identical to most other places you could use. You must set up an account before you order, but fortunately you can use your existing Apple ID for this purpose and simply enable 1-Click ordering. One thing Cyndi really likes about this process is that iPhoto only connects briefly to the Internet to access your ID information and get the OK to continue.

Sign in using your Apple ID

To order, you need an Apple ID with 1-Click® ordering enabled. Your Apple ID enables access to many Apple websites including the Apple Store, and 1-Click ordering makes checkout fast when purchasing items online.

Apple ID: picturelover@rcn.com

Password: ••••••••••

Forgot Password

Create New Apple ID   Cancel   Sign In

iPhoto looks at your pictures and puts an alert symbol next to any combination of photo and print size that your image doesn't have enough resolution to successfully print, although it doesn't actually prevent you from making that choice if you insist (**Figure 10.13**). iPhoto's alert does not appear unless the resolution problem is really severe. It only tells you when a photo will be less than adequate quality, not when it falls in the gray zone where some people will be content and others disappointed.

Kodak Print Service

| | | 4x6 prints, quantity: | 0 |
| | | 5x7 prints, quantity: | 0 |

		Size	Price	Qty
		4 x 6	$ 0.49 each	0
		5 x 7	0.99 each	0
		wallet (4)	1.79 each	0
		8 x 10	3.99 each	0
	⚠	16 x 20	14.99 each	1
	⚠	20 x 30	19.99 each	0
		4 x 6	$ 0.49 each	0
		5 x 7	0.99 each	0
		wallet (4)	1.79 each	0
		8 x 10	3.99 each	0
		16 x 20	14.99 each	0
		20 x 30	19.99 each	0

⚠ Low resolution may result in poor print quality.   4x6 Credits Remaining: 10

Figure 10.13 Pictures with alert icons in the second column don't have enough resolution to print at larger sizes. In this example, we shouldn't select a 16 x 20-inch print for this photo.

The upload time compares favorably to other online services and tells you how many pictures have been transferred as it goes. Apple tells you that your order will ship one to two days from when you upload. That translates into a delivery time similar to that of other services.

Want to use iPhoto for more than digital photos? If you've placed photos with another online service, including photos you took with traditional film and sent to the service for processing, you can just download them to your desktop and use Import to bring them into iPhoto.

iPhoto Printed Albums

Although iPhoto is smooth and convenient, it isn't the only way to get photos from your digital camera. On the other hand, it does offer one unique (as of this writing, at least!) option: You can turn any photo album you've created into a beautifully printed and bound one-of-a-kind book. What a great present for family and friends, or a wonderful way to create your own coffee-table book to display your most impressive photographic efforts.

If you want, you can click Order Book and automate the entire process. iPhoto will place each picture on its own page, with whatever name you gave the picture as a title (**Figure 10.14**).

Figure 10.14 Each page previews in the iPhoto window in sequence from left to right below the preview window. If you don't like the sequence, you can drag and drop the page thumbnails to get your preferred order.

If you'd rather have a little more control, you can choose from six different layout styles to help you customize your look, and you can decide how many pictures appear on each page within each theme.

Ordering is just as easy as getting individual photos. We were a little surprised by how expensive the added tax and shipping costs made the book, but it was hard not to be delighted by the quality of the finished product—and the delighted faces when we presented it as a gift.

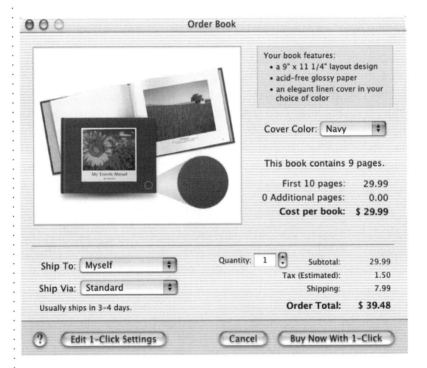

Share Your Photos

11

Is there anyone who doesn't have photos tucked away in boxes, drawers, and closets? You keep them because they're part of your history, and because you imagine that someday you'll trot them out when friends and family want pointers on great places in Mexico or Dublin or Rome. But six months later, you may not even remember the names of all of the places, or even where you put the pictures.

Remembering—and sharing your memories—gets a lot easier with digital photos. Not only can you show your pictures immediately, while everything is still fresh in your mind, but your pictures are available at any time, day or night, to anyone you want to share them with. In this chapter, we examine the growing number of options digital camera owners have for sending, displaying, and sharing their images.

Sharing without a Computer

Since digital photos are, well, digital, the best ways to share them are through some type of computer. But what do you do if you don't have a computer, or you want to share pictures with others who don't?

You can do exactly what you'd do with regular pictures, of course: print them and send copies through the mail. Most online photo services let you ship prints directly from the online site to anywhere in the world. You can have favorite photos of grandchildren placed on everything from baseball caps to greeting cards. See Chapter 10 for more on printing options, and Chapter 12 for tips on these types of photo projects.

Although expensive, a digital frame is a slick and stylish option (see Chapter 2). These are devices that look like desk or wall-mounted picture frames, and can either plug in to a wall outlet or run on standard batteries. The nice thing about digital frames is that, although they are cool techno gadgets, you don't have to know anything about technology to enjoy them. There are no digital buttons or modes to learn. They vary in size from a small, portable, battery-run version to ones big enough to display a picture at 10 x 14 inches. The smaller versions run from $175 to $400, although the really large versions cost more than some wide-screen TVs.

Slip your camera's memory card into the frame, and it displays the pictures, either one at a time or as a slow-moving digital slide show. Combine these devices with a storage device capable of holding hundreds of photos, and you get almost infinite variety and a striking conversation piece as well.

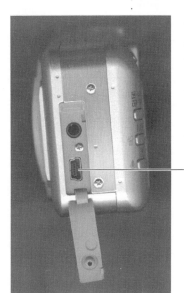

Another way to avoid using a computer to display your photos is to take advantage of your camera's capabilities. Many digital cameras have a direct video output connection and a cable that you can use to connect the camera directly to your VCR (**Figure 11.1**). Then, as the images display on the TV, you can record the photos onto videotape. (See Chapter 5.)

AV camera connector   *AV cable*

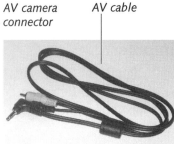

Figure 11.1 You connect the L-shaped end of the cable to your camera, then connect the other two cables to your TV or VCR to display your photos on the TV and record them.

VCRs record images in the order in which they display from the camera. If you decide to go the videotape route, use the camera's software to delete unwanted images and change the picture order before you connect to the VCR.

Emailing Your Images

The most immediate way of sharing photos computer-to-computer is to email them. They stay digital, and one electronic photo spawns dozens of copies with no effort on your part. All recent versions of email software have simple ways to attach pictures to email. Your recipient can view any JPEG file in a browser window, without additional software (**Figure 11.2**).

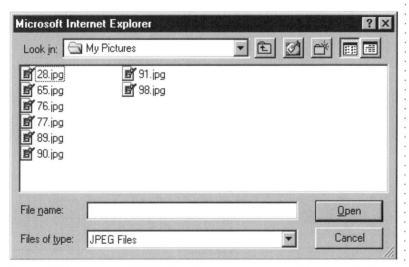

Figure 11.2 To see a JPEG in the Windows versions of Internet Explorer or Netscape, remember to change the drop-down "Files of type" menu in the Open dialog box to JPEG. Because the browser default is HTML files, you won't see any JPEG files on your computer when you browse until you change the default.

Preparing a File for Emailing

Unless you are sending lots of photos at the same time, the best type of picture file to send is JPEG. As we discussed in Chapter 7, JPEGs can be saved at different quality levels. The lower the quality, the smaller the file. But pictures can have very low quality and resolution and still look terrific onscreen.

When you attach photos to email, it pays to be considerate. The ideal combination of quality, resolution, and on-screen size for photos varies depending on the monitor screen and computer type. But you can't go wrong with most pictures if you use a resolution of 72 dpi, a quality setting of 4, and an on-screen picture size that allows the recipient to view a photo on a lower-resolution monitor without having to scroll to see part of it in a browser window. That works out to a maximum width of 740 pixels and a maximum height of 450 pixels (**Figure 11.3**).

Figure 11.3 If you make your picture too big, part of it will get cut off in the browser window. This image fits horizontally, but not vertically, requiring the viewer to scroll to see the image in its entirety.

Why Do You Need Compression?

JPEGs are already compressed files, and they're a universally accepted format. If you've prepared your pictures properly, they're the best way to send your photos. But if you plan to send dozens of JPEGs at a time, or JPEGs at a high quality for printing, you may need to gather them into folders. Since email programs can't handle folders as attachments, you'll need to compress the folder first. Additional compression is also particularly useful if you or one of your JPEG recipients uses a dial-up modem, which has a low file transfer speed.

Some people simply lower the quality of their JPEGs to be able to send them efficiently. But remember, JPEGs are a *lossy* format, which means that the color and quality you lose when you shrink their file sizes disappear forever. If you use a lossless compression utility instead, you get the benefit of temporarily smaller file sizes without losing any image quality.

Compressing Files

When you want to compress your files, first put them all in one folder on your desktop, then run the compression software on the whole folder. In Windows, you'll need software that creates ZIP files. The best-known shareware programs to do this are WinZip (www.winzip.com/) and PKZIP (www.pkware.com/). (Some computers come with WinZip installed as a trial application.) On a Macintosh, you'll need either StuffIt Deluxe or StuffIt Lite (www.stuffit.com/) to make SIT files.

Life gets a little ticklish if you are a Windows user who wants to send compressed files to a Macintosh user, or vice versa. You'll need to check with the other person first to see what software they have to decompress files, or they may not be able to view your pictures after they receive them. The company that makes StuffIt, Aladdin Systems, includes a program called DropZip in StuffIt Lite that lets you make ZIP files. The company also gives away StuffIt Expander for Windows so PC users can open Macintosh SIT files.

In both cases, if the recipient has the right software installed, the email software should prompt the decompression part of the software to go to work when the email and attachment arrive at their destination. But even if it doesn't, you can double-click the software's icon or choose the program from the Start menu and then either navigate to the compressed file or drag and drop it onto the compressor's icon for instant decompression.

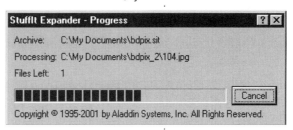

Even with compression, don't go overboard on sending large attachments. Some email systems and servers limit the size of attachments they'll deliver or receive.

Receiving Compressed Mac Files on a PC

If you send compressed files using a browser's email application (Netscape's Messenger or Microsoft's Outlook Express), be aware that each of these email programs has preselected a type of encoding and decoding to automatically decompress all compressed files you receive. Unfortunately, if you are a Windows user receiving a compressed SIT file from a Mac user, the email program will automatically decompress the files the wrong way, stripping away elements that these files need to be read properly again on any platform.

If you are a Windows user with lots of Macintosh friends (or one really good Mac friend), we recommend that you download the free version of Stuffit Expander for Windows, which will decompress both SIT and ZIP files. That way, you'll always be able to read compressed files sent to you by Macintosh users.

Attaching an Image to Email

When an email program sends attachments, it *encodes* (translates) them into a special format to send them successfully over the Internet. Unfortunately, not all email systems and computer platforms use the same method of encoding. When you send a file in one encoding scheme to an email program using a different scheme, the files become corrupted and won't open, or won't open properly.

Most current email software uses a type of encoding called MIME (Multipurpose Internet Mail Extensions) as its default. Even if your email doesn't, you should be able to change your email setting to this encoding method. If you're sending from a Macintosh email program to a Windows user, it's particularly important to locate this setting (**Figure 11.4**).

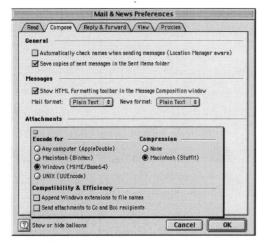

Figure 11.4 In Microsoft Entourage, you can specify encoding settings for a number of platforms.

If you'll be sending attachments on a regular basis to and from different types of computers, look in your email settings for a place where you can set the attachment encoding. In Eudora, for example, you'll find it in the Settings menu. In Microsoft Entourage, the settings are under the Compose tab in the Preferences dialog box.

Sending and Receiving Attachments in AOL

AOL's strong suit is not its email, and AOL has been very slow to bring its handling of attachments up to the level of Internet mail providers. In versions prior to 5.0, an AOL user can't send multiple photos as attachments. (Even in later versions, transmitting multiple files can sometimes cause problems.) In versions prior to 7.0, you can't send *embedded* images (images inserted within the body of the email message), except to other AOL users. And if someone from outside AOL sends you attachments without compressing them, they will become garbled and impossible to view.

So if you are an AOL user and you want to send and receive photos outside AOL, you should begin by upgrading to version 7.0. If you don't want to do that, you should compress everything you send out as an attachment. AOL uses as its email compression program whatever is standard on your platform: ZIP for Windows, SIT for Macs. Since you can't control the method of compression unless you compress your files before you use AOL's email, you should tell your recipient what type of compressed file (ZIP or SIT) they'll receive.

Online Photo Services

Online photo services are in the business of photo sharing. If they don't make it easy for you to use them, they won't be around for very long. There's no reason to settle for a service that doesn't have all the options that you like—or to limit yourself to only one service if you can't find the best combination of options. By all means, try out more than one while you're still experimenting with image sharing. You might find that one service is particularly good for special gift ideas (like making T-shirts and greeting cards) but costs more than you'd like for prints.

Uploading and Your Internet Connection

If you're using a photo service for both prints and online images, make sure that its data transfer rates are as fast as possible. To test this, sign on to two or three services you're considering, and then upload a good-quality image to each of them at a day and time you'd be likely to transfer photos. Then time the uploads. Remember that an extra 30 seconds to send one picture could mean an extra 5 minutes for 10 pictures. Just to be thorough, try again later, or on a different day. By experimenting, you'll get a realistic sense of how long you can expect to wait while uploading.

When you upload to create Web pages or photo albums, transfer speed is less important if you have first prepared the images for online-only use. That means your pictures should be 72 dpi, medium-to-low quality JPEGs. You can transfer a dozen small files in the time it will take you to upload a single high-resolution photo. If the service also offers the option for people to order prints from your online albums, be sure to warn your friends about the low quality of the images. No one will thank you if they buy five of your wedding pictures and they arrive ugly and jagged!

Using Photo Service Pages

Two of the most popular options offered by online photo services are customer Web pages and photo albums. The biggest difference between the two is that Web pages are open to the entire world. Photo albums are usually protected in some way, so that only those people you want to see them can do so. In general, photo service sites limit the display of your album to the private mailing lists you specify, because they don't want to be responsible for the type of material you post (a sensible position, we think). Although each photo service has a slightly different method and interface, in all cases the process of creating an album or Web page is easy: If you know how to upload a file, you can display your images online.

Snapfish's options are typical of most services. (See Appendix C for a selection of online photo services.) First you select an album to share, next you create a list of your recipients' email addresses, and then you create an email invitation to view your photos at the service's site (**Figure 11.5**). You set the level of access for your mailing list: You could specify that people only be able to view the pictures and order copies, or you could let them do anything with the pictures except delete them or

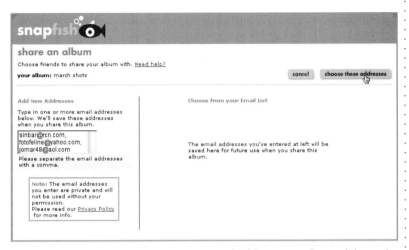

Figure 11.5 You type your recipients' email addresses, and Snapfish sends the email to all of them and saves the addresses for your future use.

edit their captions (**Figure 11.6**). If you want some people to have full access and others to have limited access, you'll need to send separate emails to each group.

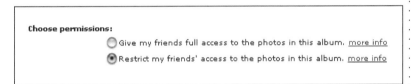

Figure 11.6 You select the radio button that offers visitors the level of access you'd like them to have to your prints.

Selecting an Online Service

Although you can use more than one service for different things, in practice most people stick with one, or at most two, favorites. You can spend a significant amount of time uploading pictures to a site, and if you use more than one site or change sites after you've uploaded, most of the time you'll have to upload all over again. So when it comes to online services, it pays to read the fine print. Some things to consider when choosing your online service:

- Are the photos secure? Sometimes we share photos with friends that we might not want everyone else in the world to see. Like cell phone conversations, material online can be vulnerable. Every reputable service should have a prominently posted security policy.

- Is the service financially stable? Although you've got a better shot with photo services supported by companies with deep pockets, it's sometimes hard to tell which ones those are. If the service is slow to respond to your questions, frequently threatens changes in pricing or policy, or doesn't inform you at all when it makes changes, you should start looking for a new service.

- Do you have to pay to use the service? Some services are only free for a trial period; after that they charge a monthly fee to store your pictures.

- Does the service have a maximum storage limit? If so, what is it? Most photo services limit the amount of space you can use to store your pictures. Three exceptions are Ofoto, Shutterfly, and PhotoAccess. But even with limited storage, if you don't post a lot of pictures or you only upload pictures at low resolution, that limited space may be unlimited for your purposes.

- Are the photos there for the foreseeable future, or will the service erase the files eventually? Some services don't limit the amount of space you can have on a server, but do limit how long you can have it there. Some services, like FotoTime, give you 30 days to decide whether or not you like their service. If you don't subscribe by the end of that period, they delete the images in your storage space (**Figure 11.7**).

How much is a FotoTime Subscription?

- We give you 30 days to try out our photo sharing service at no charge.
- You pay nothing at all to try out the service.
- If you decide to keep the service, simply buy a one year subscription for $23.95 (that's less than $2 per month) which includes 250MB of storage. If you need more space, each additional 250MB costs 23.95.
- If you decide not to subscribe, your pictures will automatically be purged from our system 30 days after you registered. Your account stays active, and you can upload pictures again, but they will be purged again 30 days later. This is perfect for those that want to order prints from FotoTime, but don't need long term storage for their pictures.
- The subscription fee is only for storage of photos on FotoTime.com. FotoAlbum remains freeware, you can use it for FREE.

Close Window

Figure 11.7 FotoTime offers excellent free album software for both the Mac and the PC. But you must pay to maintain your storage at the site.

Another thing to consider is how many functions the service offers. If you expect to make T-shirts or other gifts on a regular basis, it won't pay to use a service that doesn't make those projects easy to create.

Don't use a photo service's site as your photo backup space. Make sure that you have your photos saved on a CD as well. Services can go out of business or have technical problems, and none make any promises about liability if you lose pictures.

Using iPhoto to Share Online

iPhoto is interconnected with Apple's other "i" applications—iTunes, iMovie, and iDVD—via iTools, an online space for document storage. Simply by registering on the Apple site, you can claim a dedicated iTools space, a particularly useful step if you want to create a Web page quickly from your iPhoto images.

When you click Share, and then the HomePage button, iPhoto connects you to your online site and creates a simple grid of framed images. You can click to customize whether the pictures will be displayed with or without a frame, and which type of frame you'd like (**Figure 11.8**). Click Publish, and iPhoto uploads your photos to your iTools space, then automatically builds the Web page.

Figure 11.8 When you choose a frame type in iPhoto, all pictures use the same frame. This home page has a black frame applied to all of the thumbnail pictures. If you click one of the thumbnails, a larger image will appear.

If you'd like more control over the way your Web page looks, instead of going straight to HomePage, choose Export from the File menu. In the Export Images dialog box, choose the Web Page tab (**Figure 11.9**). Make your changes in this dialog box, then click the Export button and choose a place for the files.

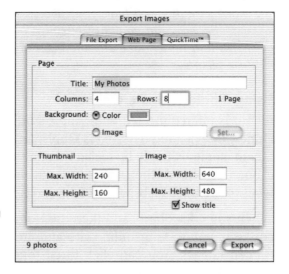

Figure 11.9 You can specify the number of picture columns and rows, select how big you want the thumbnails and full-size pictures to be, and add a complementary background color to the page.

Unlike some other online photo-developing services, iPhoto only processes digital images. But if you want to use iPhoto for image cataloging or to create a Web page, just ask the photo service that processes your film to save your pictures onto a CD. You can import the pictures from the CD into iPhoto, just like you import pictures from your camera.

Creating a Personal Web Page

It used to be that to share your photos online you needed to have your own Web site. Then you had to use Microsoft Front-Page or some other Web-page-creation software to actually create the site. In most cases, if you weren't a Web designer or techie, that requirement meant spending some serious time figuring out software and how to organize your files properly. Someone who is creating a portfolio online, or already has a Web site, will still want to build their own site in order to control the material, look, and domain name. If this describes you but you don't yet have your own Web page, we recommend

Robin Williams' and John Tollet's *Non-Designer's Web Book, Second Edition* (from Peachpit Press) for help in creating and posting your material.

If you want to share individual photos with the rest of the world but don't want to spend the time learning a new program, we recommend Yahoo GeoCities. As long as you don't need a personalized domain name, this is a great way to get started with a Web page. You can easily build a small Web site using Yahoo's templates and wizards (**Figure 11.10**). If the 15 MB of space on the free site isn't enough for all your photos, you can upgrade to different site levels for different monthly prices.

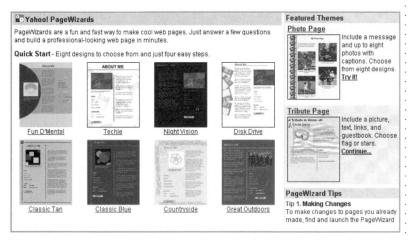

Figure 11.10 Yahoo makes it incredibly easy to create a Web site. It even has a template with eight possible variations designed specifically for photo pages.

Displaying Photos on PDAs

Imagine how cool—and impressive—it would be to show your pictures on your Palm or Pocket PC. There are a thousand possible uses: from showing pictures of your family to carrying photos to an appraiser rather than the expensive item itself. Or if you're a real estate agent, you could have pictures of an apartment or house on your PDA (personal digital assisant) to show clients. If they like what they see, you could bring them to the house. If they don't, you've saved a lot of time and mileage.

As PDAs become more like desktop computers, software can make it easy to use a PDA for these purposes. The most popular cross-platform program for the Palm OS is Club Photo's free Album To Go—a compelling reason to use their photo site (www.clubphoto.com/). The software allows you to organize albums on your computer or the service's Web site, then transfer them to your Palm handheld, just as you would with any other HotSync operation. The newest versions work only with color Palms, although there is an older, feature-limited Windows version for black-and-white PDAs. If you are a Mac user running OS X, or you have a black-and-white Palm handheld and don't want a limited application, consider Splash-Photo (www.splashdata.com/). It costs $9.95 (as opposed to the free Album To Go software), but it's worth it (**Figure 11.11**).

Figure 11.11 SplashPhoto's desktop application, which includes an image editor, offers a clear, elegant interface and does an excellent job of maintaining image quality in a very small file.

If you have a Pocket PC instead, Cresotech's PocketPoint (www.cresotech.com/) serves the same purpose. In addition, you can use it to run a presentation based on your images. Both of these PDA solutions are under $25, so there's no financial barrier to getting a whole new reason to use your PDA.

If you decide to use your PDA to display photos, you may need to adapt some of your photos. PDAs are long and narrow, while computer screens are wider and less deep. Vertical photos will hold up pretty well when you transfer them, but horizontal photos on a PDA can be really tiny. Rotating images 90 degrees before you transfer them keeps the pictures at maximum size, and it's a lot easier to turn the PDA than squint at a tiny image.

Making a Digital Slide Show

Slide shows used to require special software and preparation. Today, many photo-editing programs include an automatic slide show maker as part of their packages, and several online services offer the option for photos you've uploaded (**Figure 11.12**). Generally, you'll find that slide shows run better right on your

Figure 11.12 Microsoft lets you arrange your photos in folders and view them in a slide-show format.

hard drive than they do on the Web, where pictures will tend to display more slowly, and at a smaller size.

Most preformatted slide shows allow you to do some limited customizing. Apple's iPhoto, for example, lets you create slide shows from individual albums, or from your entire photo database. If you manually arrange the images in the album before making the slide show, they'll play in whatever order you choose. In the Preferences settings (**Figure 11.13**), you can choose how long images will remain on screen, and—not a usual slide-show option—add music from any MP3 file you have in iTunes.

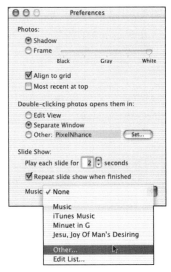

Figure 11.13 If you go to iPhoto Preferences, you can navigate to your iTunes folder and choose appropriate music to accompany your slide show.

If you're a Mac user who wants a slide show with a wider variety of options, check out iView MediaPro (www.iview-multimedia.com). Although it's inexpensive shareware, you have many options that you wouldn't ordinarily find outside a professional program. And despite its being a very capable asset management tool, you barely need any instruction to find your way around the interface. You can create a color frame for the show, add titles through captions or headlines you type in, choose size and order, and add QuickTime effects for transitions between pictures (**Figure 11.14**). You can import any type of media to iView MediaPro—images, movie clips, MP3s. You can even import files directly from your digital camera.

iView also lets you make a QuickTime movie from the same media so you can share your creation with friends. This is unusual. Most photo-editor slide shows don't have a stand-alone program for running the slide show on computers that lack the software you used to make it. In most cases, if you want to show your customized slide show, you have to do it in person.

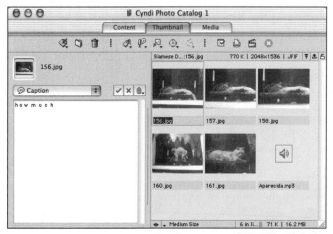

Figure 11.14 iView MediaPro offers lots of ways to make your slide show unique. You can drag and drop media onto its Thumbnail tab (left), then select a QuickTime transition and image arrangement (below left). Cyndi ended up with an arrangement called Artic Circle (below), where each image and its caption transitions every few seconds.

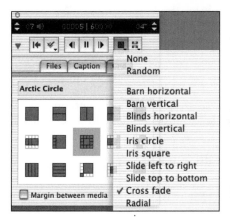

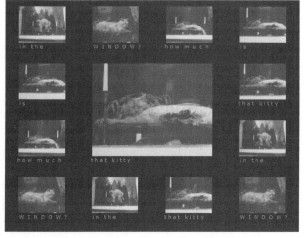

Photo Projects 12

One big difference between film photography and digital photography can be summed up in two words: instant fun.

A film image exists only as a negative and a print or slide. If you want to do something other than frame the photo, you'll have turn the picture over to a professional service or scan it into a computer. But digital photos are already in computer format. They don't cost anything to duplicate, and after fixing and altering them you can use them in almost any imaginable way: turn them into gifts or cards, or add them to movies; make art or make 'em laugh with customized gags. Or keep a clever seven-year-old busy for hours.

Interested? This chapter offers pointers on handling a range of typical projects based on your digital photos.

Make a Picture T-Shirt

Any picture you can print, you can put on a T-shirt. Although you can't print directly from your computer onto the shirt itself, you can print on special transfer paper. You can buy special paper at any store that sells your printer's regular photo paper. Or you can buy everything at one time: Epson, for instance, sells T-shirts in a wide range of sizes that you can buy when you order your transfer paper. After you've printed the photo (and any text or extras you've added) on this paper, all you have to do is iron the image onto a T-shirt or sweatshirt. Presto, you have a totally unique but inexpensive gift.

To get the most successful T-shirts with the least hassle, wash, dry, and iron the shirts before you start. Wrinkles can hamper your ability to align the photo on the shirt properly.

If you're making more than one T-shirt, all of that aligning and ironing can get tedious. And the transfers, although they provide instant gratification, are equally short lived. They begin to fade as you launder. For longer-lasting and multiple copies of your T-shirt, you might be better off using an online service that prints using silkscreening—a much more permanent and professional method that prints directly onto the fabric. And the vibrancy of the colors will be much closer to what you see onscreen than the transfer version.

Microsoft's MSN Photos (http://photos.msn.com/) will make T-shirts for you, as will iPrint (www.iprint.com) and PhotoAccess (www.photoaccess.com). All of them offer printing not only on shirts, but on caps as well. You'll barely have to do a thing besides choose the photo you want to use and the type of garment you want it placed on (**Figure 12.1**).

Figure 12.1 PhotoAccess specializes in all things photo. Besides the usual T-shirts and caps, they'll apply your photo to everything from a puzzle to the paper you wrap the present in.

Create Photo Greeting Cards

Any photo you print that meets basic postal regulations—no shorter than 3.5 inches and no wider than 6.5 inches—can be used as a postcard. We know people who create custom post-cards of places they've visited and strange things they've seen. With a little more effort, you can turn that postcard concept into a family holiday card (**Figure 12.2**), or a more formal greet-ing card. All you need is a simple print template program or an imaging program that allows you to add type to the picture.

Figure 12.2 To make this holiday picture card, we resized the image working area to leave a blank area to the right of the picture. We added type, then saved the file to print it.

If you want a professional look but don't want to learn one of the professional desktop-publishing software packages, sev-eral programs will help you get creative painlessly. We've already mentioned Microsoft's PictureIt for photo editing. But for the same price as PictureIt, you can also get Microsoft Pub-lisher—a desktop-publishing program that's easy to figure out, integrates nicely with the photo software, and has lots of wiz-ards and templates for you to fall back on. The most versatile but inexpensive program for the Mac is Print Explosion Deluxe (www.novadevelopment.com). It works on both the classic Mac and OS X, and is a great tool for any home project that com-bines photos and text.

On the other hand, if you don't want to invest the time in learning one of those programs, try MSN Photos. This site not only allows you to take a photo and combine it with one of its templates to create a greeting card, but it'll even print and mail the cards for you. Think of how much easier getting your holiday cards out could be this year.

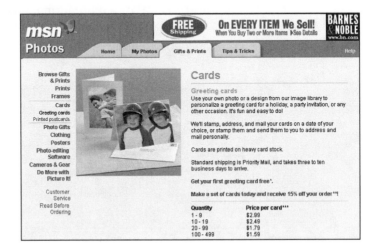

 Even though many of the functions in Microsoft Publisher that are most important to the nonprofessional exist at MSN Photos, you'll move faster and have more options if you use the full program on your own computer.

Make a Photo Panorama

If you've ever tried to shoot a panorama on a film camera and then link the prints to show them, you've probably noticed that, even when shooting using a tripod, it's next to impossible to get the linkages right. One side of the shot is often darker than the side that should attach to it, and tops and bottoms don't align.

Before digital cameras, you could scan prints or negatives into the computer, then use an image-editing program to improve the connections. But this required great skill and patience. Now, several photo-editing programs include an easy stitch function. Jasc After Shot™ allows you to drag several images into a stitch window (**Figure 12.3**), where the program will merge them for

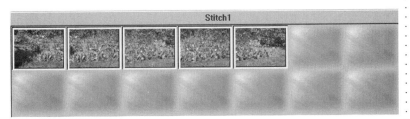

Figure 12.3 Jasc After Shot will attempt to make a panorama of the images in the Stitch window.

you. In our experience, however, automatic merges can be unsuccessful unless each image has a distinct object in it that the software can recognize to make the match (**Figure 12.4**).

Figure 12.4 This group of five images confused Jasc After Shot—it couldn't figure out which tulips matched up from image to image. As a result, the images were placed transparently one over the other instead of next to each other.

On the other hand, a photo panorama is remarkably easy to make if your camera and software are working collaboratively. Some cameras (like the Canon PowerShot series) come with a panorama setting that helps you set up your images to minimize problems. You can drag and drop images into Canon's PhotoStitch window and rearrange them if they uploaded in the wrong order. Click Start, and the program automatically matches up your pictures and merges them into one printable image, correcting color and shadow at the merges (**Figure 12.5**).

Figure 12.5 In this picture, the program displays the seam areas so you can check the program's decisions.

If your camera has this setting, it probably also has bundled-image-stitching software to help you work with your photos after you upload them. This software should trim the photo down to one seamless rectangle and allow you to export the merged photo as one file for printing or uploading.

Stitch Witchery

No matter what camera and software you use, your original images must be suitable for stitching together. You can do a lot during shooting to improve the end result of your stitched panorama. Some hints for preparation:

- Use a tripod if you can. If you don't have one, try to stay as still as possible while you shoot. Stand with your feet apart and rotate your upper body only.

- When you compose your shots, try to create a baseline—a horizontal place in the image that you can treat as the bottom of each shot.

- Overlap. At least one-third of the material in one photo should appear in the next one as well. Half is even better.

- Try to shoot in dependable lighting. If the sun is going in and out of clouds, try to take your pictures at a time when every shot will have about the same brightness.

Stitching is memory-intensive, because the stitching program needs to have several images available at the same time. The more images, and the higher their resolution, the longer stitching will take. If your computer doesn't have a lot of memory, stitching can take a very long time, or even fail to complete. For example, on a fast computer, a stitch of five images can take less than ten seconds. The same stitch on a slower computer can take as long as five minutes.

Check your camera documentation before shooting images you'll want to stitch together. There may be a maximum number of photos you can shoot to create a panorama.

Use Your Photos for Auctions

The digital camera is the perfect tool for advertising things on eBay or other auction sites. But it pays to set up your shot properly and edit your picture if you want to up your chances of getting the most interest in an item. Creating a photo for an auction is not much different than preparing it for any other online use: You need to pick the right photo, get it onto your computer, then get the photo to the auction site.

Start by creating the right setting for your photo. If the subject is small enough, put a contrasting background behind it before you shoot, and make sure that the object is the only thing in the photo (**Figure 12.6**). You can shoot at a low resolution, because your final image will be seen onscreen, but make sure that the object is sharply in focus. Edit out any-

Figure 12.6 On the left, a good shot of an object for sale. It will be easy to edit and post. On the right, a confusing shot. Which of these things is for sale? You'll have to edit the other objects out of the picture—more work than should be necessary.

thing that might distract from the main attraction. Save the edited file with a name that describes exactly what the object is; this is particularly important if you're selling more than one thing at a time.

You want your image to download quickly, because if it doesn't the prospective buyer will move on to someone else's item. Aim for a file size of 30 to 40 kilobytes for your JPEG file. Smaller is even better if the photo still looks good when you're done. You may have to experiment a little before you find the right combination of JPEG quality and picture dimensions, so be sure to keep a copy of the original picture in case you go too far and lose image quality.

Last step: uploading the file. eBay and other sites let you upload directly to their servers. Alternatively, you could create a photo-service site that contains pictures of all the things you have for sale. If you're selling a lot of household goods because you're moving, for example, having all of them on one page might prompt people to buy more than one item at a time. Upload your files to the photo service, then provide the access information as part of the auction info.

Customize Your Computer Desktop

Digital photography is great for sharing photos, but sometimes we also like to do things just for ourselves. We like to set our own environment, surrounded by our favorite things. That's the reason we display family or vacation pictures on our desks. Your digital photos can take their places on your computer desktop in the same way. You can make them a permanent part of your desktop appearance by placing them on the screen's background or turning them into personal screensavers. Although every operating system has a different set of require-ments and methods, they all make it easy for you to add your photos to their look and feel.

Create Desktop Backgrounds

If you know how to change a picture's resolution and size (see Chapter 8 for more information), you're only a few steps away from having that picture as your personal wallpaper.

On every OS, your first step is to check what resolution you are currently using on your screen. If you choose an image of the wrong resolution, the picture on your desktop can look blurry when it's stretched to fill the entire screen. In Windows, you right-click on the desktop and select Properties. From Display Properties, you choose the Settings tab. On the classic Mac, you open the Monitors control panel. In OS X, you click the Displays icon in System Preferences (**Figure 12.7**).

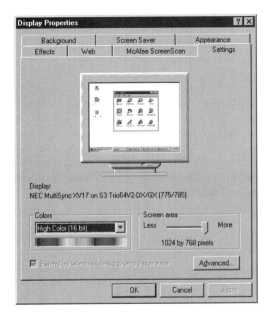

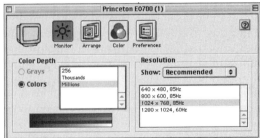

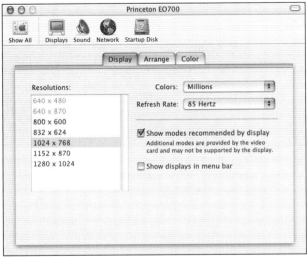

Figure 12.7 Three ways to change your display resolution: Windows, classic Mac, and Mac OS X.

On a PC, open your chosen photo in an image-editing program (photo-editing programs probably won't be able to do this) and change the file format to BMP. BMP is the Windows system format (see Chapter 7). It's the only picture format that Windows will allow you to put in the background. Change the pixel dimensions of the file to whatever your monitor resolution is. Save the file with a new name, and put it in the Windows folder on your C: drive (**Figure 12.8**).

Figure 12.8 The BMP file will be easiest to keep track of and to replace if it lives with all the other wallpaper options in your Windows folder.

Return to Display Properties, and choose the Background tab. Browse through the wallpaper choices until you see your background listed. Select it, then choose how you'd like to display it: centered, tiled, or stretched. Centered places the photo in the middle of the screen with the background framing it (**Figure 12.9**). Tiled duplicates the image as many times as necessary to fill the screen, and stretched takes the image and enlarges it to fill the background (**Figure 12.10**). Click Apply, and be delighted.

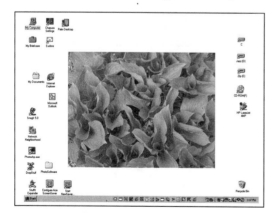

Figure 12.9 This image makes a lovely centerpiece on the desktop.

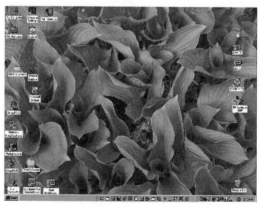

Figure 12.10 This image was shot at 640 x 480 resolution. When stretched to fill the entire screen, the image blurs.

Macs don't need a special file format. JPEGs are welcome, as long as you move them to the right place. On a classic Mac, you open the System folder and then the Appearance folder.

Drag your JPEG to the Photos folder, then open the Appearance control panel. You'll need to click the monitor icon, then click the Place Picture button. Select your JPEG from the Open dialog box, and it will appear as a preview in the Appearance dialog box. Click Set Desktop.

On Mac OS X, creating a background is even easier. Select System Preferences, then click Desktop. Find a picture file (it can be a JPEG, TIF, or even PICT) and drag it to the Preview box. The image will appear immediately on your screen. If you have two monitors, you can set different images on each screen.

You can drag a picture directly from iPhoto's thumbnails right into the Desktop dialog box.

Create Your Own Screensaver

On Mac OS X, the ability to create custom screensavers is built right into the operating system. In System Preferences, choose the Screen Saver icon. In the dialog box, select Slide Show from the Screen Savers list. If you have any picture files already in your Pictures folder, they'll begin to display in the Preview box. Click the Test button to see the slide show full screen.

By default, the screensaver will display every image in your Pictures folder, no matter what subfolder they reside in inside that folder. If you use iPhoto, every image in its catalog will display in your slide show, because iPhoto's Library folder is in the Pictures folder. To limit your slide show to specific images, create a new folder and copy the images you want to use in the slide show into it. In the Screen Saver dialog box, click the Configure button (**Figure 12.11**) and navigate to select this new folder.

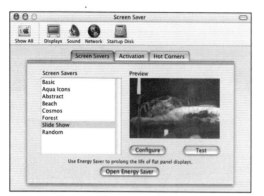 

Figure 12.11 When we set up our custom slide show in System Preferences (left), we selected our new folder, called SlideShow (right), as the source folder.

Since there's no built-in feature for the classic Mac, you're pretty limited unless you're a designer or other graphics professional who already knows your way around QuickTime and Macromedia products. If you're not, there's Blinky (www.macscreensavers.com/), a program that works a little bit like the Mac OS X screensaver. You drag and drop JPEGs to Blinky's Pictures folder, and it plays them for you. No sound, no clever transitions, but you do get to see your pictures when your Mac goes to sleep.

Windows XP's screensaver feature is similar to that of Mac OS X; in Display Preferences, click the Screen Saver tab, and use the pop-up menu to select your folder full of pictures to display. To create a screensaver for older versions of Windows, you'll need to buy additional software. Since you have to pay extra for it, you ought to expect more options and features. Expectations and results match when you use Ace Screensaver

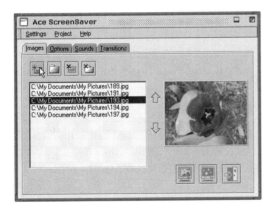

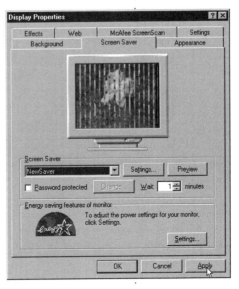

Figure 12.12 Once you've chosen your images, sounds, and transitions in the Ace Screensaver dialog box (left), you use the software to transform them into a screensaver that you can select in Display Properties (right).

(www.zbsoft.net/) to add transition effects between images, and music from your favorite MP3 file. Just click to add files to either the Images or the Sounds tab, and select between dozens of transition effects (**Figure 12.12**).

If you want to make screensavers for use on more than one platform, or if you think you've made a screensaver worth selling on the Internet, you'll need different (and somewhat more expensive) software.

Shoot Movies with Your Camera

Although some digital cameras come with a movie function that integrates motion and sound, we don't recommend that you rely on your still digital camera for this purpose. Movie and still cameras are optimized to do related but actually quite different things.

But there are certainly times when you're caught without a video camera and desperately want to show something as it moves or changes. If you do, bear in mind that there just isn't enough storage space on a Flash card or even a micro-drive to adequately record a movie. And the movies you can make with a digital camera will be extremely limited in on-screen size (usually a tiny window) and length (a couple

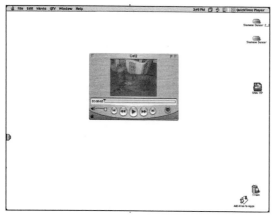

Figure 12.13 This tiny window is all you get when you shoot a movie with a digital camera.

of minutes at most) (**Figure 12.13**). If you choose to shoot at a window size large enough to actually see something, you'll measure your movie in seconds, not minutes.

You'll also need special software to view your movie: usually QuickTime, a standard on Macs but not on Windows computers. So you may need to download software after you shoot. Also bear in mind that you will have very poor sound quality. With so little storage space, a digital camera records sound in only one channel—OK for speech recorded close to the microphone, but pretty useless for music or distant voices.

Make a Movie with iPhoto

Although shooting a movie with your camera produces limited and unsatisfying results, creating a simple QuickTime movie from the photos you've stored in iPhoto is easy indeed. To create a QuickTime movie, sort your images by keyword or name, or open an album and select the ones you want to use. Click the Share button, then the Export icon below it.

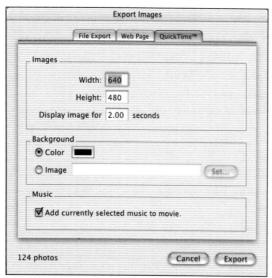

In the Export Images dialog box, choose the QuickTime tab, then click Export. In the Export Images menu, you'll be able to choose a name for the movie and where you want it stored.

The result looks very much like a slide show. The big difference is that, unlike the slide show, your movie is portable. You can send it to a friend, post it on a Web site, and copy it to a different computer—even a classic Mac or PC—as long as the receiving computer has Apple's free QuickTime player installed.

If you have Apple's QuickTime Pro or iView MediaPro, you can export your iPhoto movie as a DV stream, then import it into iMovie. There you can make it part of a movie project, adding music, transitions, and video clips.

Add Sound to Your Images

Cyndi takes a lot of pictures on vacation. Sometimes she remembers to write down the name of that cathedral, or the charming man who juggled swords in Tuscany, or the name of that showy desert flower blooming in an Arizona spring. Most of the time, however, she doesn't—and regrets it bitterly.

That's why she got a camera with a sound annotation function—and thinks you might want to, as well. With a sound function, you can verbally label a picture after you shoot it. Adding sound is usually straightforward: You just turn on the record function while looking at the photo you want to annotate, and talk into the microphone on the camera. The sound file is added to your storage card just like a photo. You can transfer it right to your desktop when you transfer your images (**Figure 12.14**).

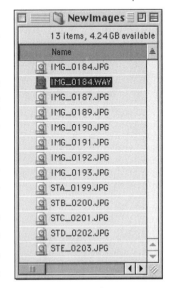

Figure 12.14 When you drag image files from your storage card to your desktop, you can drag your sound annotation file (the WAV file) as well.

Don't confuse adding sound annotation to an image with shooting a movie with sound. Movie sound and image need to be recorded at the same time. You can't return to a movie you've shot and replace or add to its sound track in the camera.

Digital Camera Troubleshooting

Even the best digital cameras can give you problems some-times. Most of these problems are easily solved. Many times the source of a problem is as simple as weak batteries or an incorrectly set option. In rare cases, there may be something wrong with the camera that requires a professional repair job.

One of the first places to look when you're experiencing a prob-lem is the camera's manual. There has been a trend in recent years for manufacturers to include only a simplified printed manual; you get the full instructions in electronic form on the CD that comes with the camera.

Here are some of the most common problems you'll encounter:

Camera won't turn on

You'll run into this problem remarkably often. Fortunately, the answer is nearly always weak batteries. Putting in fresh bat-teries usually does the trick.

If you think the batteries are OK and the camera still won't turn on, check that the batteries are inserted correctly, with each battery facing the right direction.

It's also possible that even a brand new battery is bad. Try a different set of batteries just to make sure.

If you own a camera with a lithium battery, place it in its battery charger and see whether the charger indicates that the battery is already drained. Many times, people with spare batteries put the wrong one in the camera by mistake.

Camera won't take a picture

Check that there's enough room on the storage card to take more pictures. If not, either swap out the card or delete some shots to make room.

Some cameras won't take a picture if there isn't enough light and the flash isn't ready. Look at the LED (indicator) lights on the back of the camera. If one is flashing, that usually means the camera doesn't like something about your shot. Check the manual to see what the lights mean.

Pictures are consistently under- or over-exposed

Some cameras retain exposure or flash compensation settings even after being turned off. Check these settings. Also, it's easy to accidentally hit a button on the back of the camera that changes settings.

Pictures are consistently out of focus

The most common reason for this problem is that the camera is set to Macro Focus. Check the display to see that the setting is correct.

Pictures have small distortions when enlarged

Because most digital cameras have small lenses, even a tiny fingerprint or dirt speck can loom large in a photo. Make sure that the lens is clean and dust-free. Never clean a lens with anything other than lens tissue. Paper towels and even tissues can easily scratch the lens.

Storage card can't be read

This is a common problem in cameras that use SmartMedia cards. Because the contacts on SmartMedia cards are exposed, they can get fingerprints or other shmutz on them that will prevent the camera from reading the card. Gently rub the contacts with a rubber pencil eraser. This will usually get the card up and running.

Sometimes a storage card gets corrupted and needs to be reformatted. Check your camera's instructions for formatting cards. Keep in mind that reformatting a card wipes out any stored pictures.

When all else fails

If none of the suggestions above rectify the problem, you may need to have the camera serviced. This nearly always requires you to return the camera to the manufacturer. Check with the company for instructions on where and how to ship your camera for service. Never send a camera without getting shipping instructions first, and always insure the shipment.

Image
Editing
Troubleshooting

Every image is unique. But the types of problems that arise around them often are not—especially for people who are new to image editing. Most of the time the problems are easy to correct, with a little experience and knowledge. Here are some of the most common issues and their solutions.

If your problem isn't listed here, it may be specific to your application's tools. Look at the online Help file if there is one; or when all else fails, you can bite the bullet and RTFM—Read The (Fabulous) Manual.

The wrong application opens when I double-click an image

Files are associated with specific applications in your computer. Try starting your image editing software first; then use File > Open to open your file.

My image doesn't appear in my editing application's Open menu

If you're running Windows, you probably need to change the setting in your drop-down File Type menu to All Files. If you're using Mac OS X, perhaps your file is in a format that your editing software doesn't recognize. Look to see if your file has an extension (like .jpg or .tif) at the end of its name. (To see hidden extensions in OS X, select the file and choose File > Show.) If there's no extension to be found, try simply double-clicking the file to see if a different application launches. Once the file is open, you can go to most applications' Save As dialog box and see the listed file type, which should be the current one for the image.

The red eye tool not only removes the red but also changes the eye color to gray

Red eye tools *desaturate* (change from color to grayscale) anything they identify as the eye's pupil. Before you apply the tool, zoom up to the highest enlargement so that you can limit the area that you touch. If your red eye tool is applied with a brush, change the brush to one with a smaller diameter.

The magic wand selects too much

Many magic wand tools have preferences you can set to determine how similar pixels have to be. Lower the default preference amount until your magic wand selects about the right range of pixels.

The magic wand won't select adjacent areas that are different colors

Actually, the magic wand *can* select very different things at the same time, but you have to do the selecting in stages. Try selecting the first area as usual; then, while the first area is still selected, Shift-click in the second color area.

When I try to select, I get error messages saying that I haven't selected anything

Are you using a program with layers? You may not realize that your image has more than one layer because you didn't make one yourself. But if you have copied all or part of another image into your picture, or selected a part of your picture and copied it to another place in the image, the program may have created a layer automatically. If so, the layer that is currently selected in the program is probably not the one that holds the portion of the image you are trying to select. Look at your list of layers, choose the one that you need, and try again.

I can't copy one image into another to combine them

Some programs don't let you combine two images if they're not the same color mode—for example, if one is grayscale and the other is in RGB color. Change the grayscale image to the same mode as the color one. Don't worry—the grayscale image will still look the same as it did before, but you will now be able to combine the two pictures.

When I put pieces of two images together, they didn't blend well

In some programs, selections can be done two ways: with or without anti-aliasing. Look at the preferences for your selection tool, and if the option exists, check anti-aliasing. Alas, most programs won't let you apply anti-aliasing after the fact, so you may have to redraw.

Online Resources

C

The digital camera revolution is covered extensively in the online world. The World Wide Web is a phenomenal resource for buying info, reviews, opinions, comparison shopping, and software updates.

Every major camera manufacturer has a Web site with detailed specs, FAQs, troubleshooting tips, and software updates.

Resource sites

To find a host of resource sites, go to the search engine of your choice (like www.google.com/), type *digital camera*, and you'll be delighted with the range of hints, tricks, and community you find.

Here are some of our favorites:

www.dcresource.com/

The Digital Camera Resource Page is one of the most popular sites for comprehensive information about digital photography. In addition to extensive reviews and buying guides, there are message boards, links to manufacturers and reseller's Web sites, and news.

www.dcviews.com/

DCViews offers tutorials, news, and reviews. The buying guide is organized according to price, features, and manufacturer.

www.shortcourses.com/

ShortCourses is a great Web resource for tutorials, photo galleries, and an extensive library of downloadable software.

www.megapixel.net/

Megapixel.net is a monthly online magazine that covers the digital photography world. It includes classified ads, editorials, and reviews, as well as a Price Search feature.

www.digital-camerastore.com/

Digital Camera Buyers Guide delivers what the name promises: Its extensive buying guide offers price and feature comparisons and links to online resellers. You can also sign up for the monthly email newsletter.

Photo services

Several online photo services stand out from the crowd. Here are our picks, and what we liked about them:

www.clubphoto.com/

Club Photo doesn't just take your photos and spit them out. It sees your photos as part of a process and offers lots of value in both money and extras. Most important is its family of free software. We especially like Album To Go, which is an excellent way to view images on your Palm handheld, and as well as the iShare Photoshop plug-in (works for Photoshop Elements, too) that lets you upload to Club Photo directly from Photoshop.

www.apple.com/iphoto/

iPhoto runs only on OS X. If that's your operating system, you'll be happy with both the upload times (remarkably fast) and the overall image quality of the prints you receive. Equally important, you'll find it easy to share the photos you've uploaded.

www.photos.msn.com/

We think of this site as the digest version of PictureIt. Microsoft has done a nice job of making photo projects accessible and practically foolproof. It can be a busy site at prime time because it offers so many options, so you may need a little patience on uploads. Although you can get to the Web site from any platform, nothing really works if you are using a Mac. Run Windows or walk away.

www.ofoto.com/

A generous attitude toward storage space puts Ofoto among our top picks. It doesn't purge your files, even if you don't buy prints. But you should, because the prices are competitive and the quality is high. The site also has a speedy transfer rate—something other sites can only dream of.

www.photoaccess.com/

A good competitor for Ofoto, PhotoAccess also offers unlimited free file storage. It ranks at the top for its gift catalog, which is broad, well organized, and reasonably priced.

www.snapfish.com/

Excellent prices, good-quality prints, and a friendly and usable look and feel make Snapfish a fine choice.

Index

NUMBERS

1-, 2-, 3-, and 4-megapixel cameras, 14
4 x 6-inch photo, printed by photo service, 154

A

AC adapters, 20
ACD Systems FotoCanvas, 117
ACDSee, 76
Ace Screensaver, 202–203
Adobe Photoshop, 81, 94
    magic wand tool, 112, 113
    proprietary file format of, 101
    Sharpen Edges tool, 128
    specifying memory for, 83
Adobe Photoshop Elements, 92
    cloning tool, 125
    cropping tool, 126
    File Browser window, 69
    Fill Flash tool, 117
    Hue/Saturation dialog box, 142
    Image Size dialog box, 130
    Layer via Copy tool, 150
    Levels dialog box, 118
    Picture Package option, 165–166
    proprietary file format of, 101
    red-eye reduction tool in, 113
    Sharpen Edges tool, 128
    specifying memory for, 83
    Unsharp Mask, 128
    Variations dialog box, 110
After Shot. *See* Jasc After Shot
Album To Go, 188
alkaline batteries, 19
anti-aliasing, 213
AOL, attachments in, 181
aperture
    adjusting shutter speed and, 38–39
    defined, 4

aperture priority, 49
Apple iPhoto photo service
    organizing photos with, 74–76
    printed albums, 173–174
    printing services of, 169, 170
Apple iPhoto software
    editing with, 86–87
    making movies with, 204–205
    Screen Saver dialog box, 202
    music to accompany photos in, 189
    sharing photos with, 185–186
ArcSoft PhotoImpression, 92–93, 113
aspect ratio, 133
attaching files, 180–181
autoexposure. *See also* exposure
    about, 48
    exposure compensation, 50
    shooting against the light, 36–38
autofocus. *See also* focus
    about, 16, 46
    overriding, 33
    using with zoom feature, 32
automatic mode, 15–16
AV cable, 176
AV camera connector, 176

B

backing up photos stored online, 185
batteries, 18–20
    AC adapters vs., 20
    battery packs, 20
    disposing of, 19
    film vs. digital camera, 6
    minimizing display to extend life of, 61
    types of, 18–19
battery packs, 20
Blinky, 202

BMP (bitmap) files, 100, 200
borders, 134
brightness
    adjusting, 116–117, 138–139
    of teeth, 146
brightness/contrast sliders
    defined, 116
    editing with, 138
    vs. levels tools, 117, 139
Brownie, 2
brushes and cloning, 148
buying digital cameras, 13–22
    checking auto and manual modes,
        15–16
    comparing resolution and mexapixels,
        13–14
    comparing storage media, 20–22
    Digital Camera Buyers Guide Web site,
        216
    shopping and comparing prices, 16–18
buying extras, 23–27
    camera bags, 23
    digital albums, 26, 176
    lenses, 23–24
    purchasing filters, 24
    selecting batteries, 18–20
    tripods, 24–25

C

camera bags, 23
camera obscura, 2
cameras. *See* digital cameras; film cameras
captions, 135
card readers. *See also* storage cards; flash
    cards
    about, 22
    built into inkjet printers, 155
    connecting to computer, 63
cartridges for inkjet printers, 157–159
cataloging software, 74–76
CD burners, 12
CDs
    archiving original photos on, 73–74
    backing up photos stored with online
        photo services, 185
    burning images on, 73–74
    storing images on, 12
center weighting, 36

channels
    changing levels to adjust color shifts,
        142–144
    defined, 115
cloning tools
    overview, 124–125
    removing wrinkles with, 145–147
    tips for using, 148
Club Photo, 188, 216
color
    correcting shifts in, 141–144
    digital photography and, 4–5
    film photography and, 4
Color It!. *See* MicroFrontier Color It!
commercial image editors, 90–92
CompactFlash cards, 21
composing photographs, 27–41. *See also*
    framing photos; light; portraits
    avoiding framing problems, 30–31
    choosing optimum distance, 32–33
    directing attention with focus, 33
    eliminating glare from flash, 54–55, 56
    framing photos, 29–30
    f-stop and shutter speed, 38–39
    gauging light source, 35–36
    portraits, 41
    Rule of Thirds, 34
    setting up shots, 28–29
    shooting against light, 36–38
    shooting objects in motion, 39–40
    working with available light, 34–35
compression
    about, 178–179
    JPEG file, 105–107
    LZW, 105
    software for, 179–180
computers. *See also* Macintosh; Microsoft
    Windows
    adding USB port to, 62
    card readers for, 22
    connecting camera to, 61–64
    creating desktop backgrounds, 198–201
    making personalized screensaver on,
        201–203
    moving photos from flash card to, 65–66
    organizing to store images, 64
    preparing for use with digital camera, 8–9
    transferring photos to, 64–68

USB ports and connectors, 10–11
viewing transferred photos on, 68–69
connecting camera to computer, 61–64
connecting card reader to computer, 63
USB connections, 61–62
using direct connections, 62
constraining
image proportions, 133
image size, 131
contrast
adjusting, 116–117, 138–139
brightness and contrast sliders vs. levels
tools, 139
creating visual interest with, 38
Corel Photo-Paint, 94
costs
of film vs. digital cameras, 6
of inkjet printers, 155
shopping for best prices, 16–18
cropping tools, 126
Curves dialog box, 119
curves tool, 119

D

DCViews Web site, 216
deleting unwanted photos, 61, 177
desktop backgrounds, 198–201
developer, 3
digital albums, 26, 176
Digital Camera Buyers Guide Web site, 216
Digital Camera Resource Page, 215
digital cameras. *See also* digital photography;
image editing; setting camera features
AC adapters for, 20
checking auto and manual modes, 15–16
comparing resolution and mexapixels,
13–14
connecting to computer, 61–64
filters, 24
megapixels, 13–14
online resources for, 215–217
optical vs. digital zoom, 15, 51–52
preparing computer for use with, 8–9
printing photos from, 157
resolution settings, 43–45
returning to manufacturer, 209
selecting battery types, 18–20
setting JPEG quality choices for, 97,
105–107

shooting movies with, 203–205
shutter latency, 5
size of, 8
storage media for, 20–22
technology of, 4–5
troubleshooting, 207–209
USB ports and connectors for, 10–11
view of common buttons and features on,
45
digital frames, 26, 176
digital photography. *See also* digital cameras
choosing editing software, 78–80
evolution of, 2–3
film photography vs., 5–8
digital slide shows, 188–190
Digital Wallet, 25–26
digital zoom, 15, 51–52
disk space
editing software and, 82
size of photos and, 64
storing images on CDs and, 12
display
illustrated, 45
minimizing use of, 61
disposing of batteries, 19
distortions in enlarged photos, 208
dither, 157
documenting online sale items, 197–198
Dodge and Burn tools
editing with Dodge tool, 147–148
using, 119–120, 148
downloading images
on eBay, 198
from storage cards, 25–26
drop-and-crop software, 84–87. *See also*
specific software by name
duplicating digital images, 7
dye-sublimation printers, 155

E

editing software, 77–94. *See also* image
editing; *and specific software by name*
choosing, 78–80
drop-and-crop, 84–87
freeware and shareware vs. commercial,
79–80
image editors, 81, 87–92
memory requirements and, 82–83
overview, 77–78

editing software (*continued*)
    photo editors, 92–94
    professional editing software, 94
    saving original and edited copies of
        photos, 103
    summary of types of, 80–82, 84
emailing images, 177–181
    about compression, 178–179
    attaching files, 180–181
    compressing files, 179–180
    file size and, 180
    overview, 177
    preparing files, 177–178
    sending and receiving attachments in
        AOL, 181
emulsion
    defined, 3
    layers of color film, 4
encoded files, 180–181
Epson inkjet printers, 158–159
equipment. *See* buying digital cameras
erasing
    flash card, 66–67
    large objects, 148–150
Export Images dialog (iPhoto), 186, 204
exposure, 47–51. *See also* autoexposure
    aperture priority and, 49
    correcting with white balance, 50–51
    exposure compensation, 50
    how autoexposure works, 48
    manual, 49
    setting shutter priority, 48–49
    shooting against the light and automatic,
        36–38
    troubleshooting consistent problems, 208
exposure compensation, 50
exposure LED, 45
extended warranties for cameras, 18
external flash option, 53

F

file compression software, 179–180
file formats, 95–107. *See also* JPEG files; TIFF
    files
    BMP, 100, 200
    changing, 102–107
    choosing image, 95–96
    JPEG, 96–97, 170

    Mac and Windows system, 100
    proprietary, 101–102
    RAW, 98–100
    TIFF, 98, 104–105
    Web graphics formats, 100–101
File Browser window (Photoshop Elements),
    69
files. *See also* file formats; JPEG files; TIFF
    files
    adjusting brightness and contrast on
        duplicate, 138
    attaching image, 180–181
    BMP, 100, 200
    choosing resolution settings for JPEG, 44
    compression of, 178–179
    preparing for emailing, 177–178
    renaming transferred photos, 71
    saving and clearing history of undos, 83
    saving in JPEG format, 105–107
    saving in TIFF format, 104–105
    saving original and edited copies of, 103
    size of emailed images, 180
fill flash, 53–54
film cameras. *See also* film photography
    cost of, 6
    size of, 8
    storage capacity and, 5–6
    technology of, 3–4
film photography. *See also* film cameras
    digital photography vs., 5–8
    technology of, 3–4
filters, 24
FireWire ports, 12
flash, 52–56
    about, 52–53
    avoiding harsh lighting of, 32–33
    eliminating glare from flash, 54–55, 56
    external, 53
    fill, 53–54
    night settings for, 55
    reducing red eye, 53
    shooting without, 54–55
flash cards
    erasing, 66–67
    extra, 25
    moving photos to computers from, 65–66
    swapping, 67–68
    turning off Macintosh File Sharing before
        ejecting, 68

flash LED, 45
flash settings button, 45
focus, 45–47
    autofocus, 16, 32, 33, 46
    automatic and manual lens, 15–16
    of background images with zoom feature,
        32
    choosing optimum distance for, 32–33
    directing attention with, 33
    macro, 47
    manual, 47
    overview, 45
    problems with, 208
folders, organizing, 72–73
FotoCanvas, 117
FotoTime photo service, 184
framing photos
    avoiding problems, 30–31
    eliminating distracting elements by, 29–30
    portraits, 41
    Rule of Thirds, 34
freeware. *See also* Apple iPhoto software
    defined, 79
    drop and crop, 84–87
    image editors, 88–89
    vs. commercial software, 79–80
freezing motion, 40
f-stop and shutter speed, 38–39
FuturePaint, 89–90

G

gauging light source, 35–36
general-purpose vs. photo printers, 155–157
GeoCities, 187
GIF (Graphics Interchange Format) files, 100, 101
GIMP (Gnu Image Manipulation Program),
    88–89, 128
GraphicConverter, 93–94, 110
greeting cards, 193–194

H

hardware. *See also* buying digital cameras;
    computers; storage cards
    adding USB port to computer, 62
    card readers, 22, 63, 155
    checking requirements for computer, 9
    comparing camera features and prices,
        16–18
connecting camera to computer, 61–64
selecting camera batteries, 18–20
home printing of photos, 153–154
hot spots, 110
hue, contrast, and brightness, 115–117
Hue/Saturation dialog box (Photoshop
    Elements), 142
Hue/Saturation slider, 141–143

I

icons, 102
IEEE 1394 ports, 12
image editing, 109–136, 137–152. *See also*
    editing software; image editors
    adding borders, 134
    adding captions, 135
    adjusting brightness and contrast, 138–139
    changing image resolution and size,
        132–133
    changing print resolution and size,
        130–131
    checking software's tools for, 111
    cloning tools, 124–125
    correcting color shifts, 141–144
    cropping tools, 126
    curves tool, 119
    Dodge and Burn tools, 119–120
    erasing large objects, 148–150
    guidelines for making multiple
        corrections, 135
    hue, contrast, and brightness, 115–117
    knowing what to fix, 109–111
    layers and, 120–122
    levels tools, 117–118, 139, 140–141
    magic wand tool, 112, 113, 151, 212
    masks, 123, 151–152
    red-eye-reduction tools, 113–115
    removing wrinkles and blemishes,
        144–148
    selection tools for, 112–113
    sharpening tools, 127–129
    troubleshooting, 212–213
image editors, 81, 87–92
    commercial, 90–92
    freeware, 88–89
    Open menu, 212
    overview, 87
    selection errors, 212–213

Image Size dialog box (Photoshop Elements), 130
images. *See* photographs
image-stitching software, 196–197
infrared transfer connections, 66
inkjet printers, 154–160
    cartridges for, 157–159
    general-purpose vs. photo quality, 155–157
    increasing longevity of inkjet prints, 163
    maintaining, 159–160
    paper for, 160–164
Internet. *See also* Web sites
    online digital camera resources, 215–217
    uploading image files to, 182
iPhoto. *See* Apple iPhoto software
iPhoto photo service. *See* Apple iPhoto photo service
ISO settings, 40
iView MediaPro, 189–190

J

Jasc After Shot, 87, 113, 195
Jasc Paint Shop Pro, 81, 91–92, 116
JPEG (Joint Photographic Experts Group) files
    choosing resolution settings for, 44
    features of, 96–97
    optimized and progressive, 107
    photo services' preference for, 170
    quality levels for, 97
    saving files in, 105–107

K

Kiosks, printing, 168
Kodak print service, 169, 172

L

laptops
    adding USB port to, 62
    card readers for, 22
Layer via Copy tool (Photoshop Elements), 150
layers
    image editing and, 120–122
    memory requirements, 82
    selecting objects on, 212–213

Layers palette, 120, 121
LCD display. *See* display
lens cleaner, 25
lenses. *See also* focus
    automatic and manual focusing of, 15–16
    cleaning, 25
    optical vs. digital zooming, 15, 51–52
    purchasing additional, 23–24
Levels histogram, 140, 143, 144
levels tools, 117–118
    adjusting images with, 139–141
    brightness and contrast sliders vs., 117, 139
    correcting color shifts, 142–144
light
    gauging source of, 35–36
    for outdoor shots, 36
    photography without flash, 54–55
    shooting against, 36–38
    softening flash lighting, 32–33
    working with available, 34–35
lithium batteries, 18–19, 20
local printing services, 168
longevity of inkjet prints, 163
lossy format, 97
lubricating print head of printers, 160
LZW compression, 105

M

Macintosh
    changing display resolution, 199
    connecting camera to computer, 62
    creating desktop backgrounds, 200–201
    Epson cleaning utility for, 159
    File Sharing, 68
    iPhoto printing services, 169, 171–174
    sending compressed files to Windows users, 179, 180
    swapping flash cards, 67–68
    system file types, 100
macro focus, 47
macro focus/delete button, 45
magic wand tool
    about Photoshop, 112, 113
    selection problems with, 151, 212
mail order shopping, 17–18

maintaining printers, 159–160
manual exposure, 49
manual focus, 47
manual focus button, 45
manual mode, 15–16
masks, 123, 151–152
Megapixel.net online magazine, 216
megapixels
    chart of print sizes and suggested
        resolutions, 165
    comparing camera models using, 14
    defined, 4
    resolution and, 13
Memory Sticks, 22
menu button, 45
menu control buttons, 45
MicroFrontier Color It!, 91, 128
Microsoft Entourage, 180, 181
Microsoft Internet Explorer, 177
Microsoft Picture It!
    MSN Photos and, 192, 194
    photo editing with, 193
    software, 85, 93
    wizards in, 111
Microsoft Publisher, 193, 194
Microsoft Windows
    changing display resolution, 199
    creating desktop backgrounds, 198–200,
        202
    received compressed files from Mac users,
        179, 180
    StuffIt Expander for Windows, 179, 180
    system file types for, 100
MIME (Multipurpose Internet Mail
    Extensions), 180
monopods, 25, 55
motion shoots, 39–40
MSN Photos, 192, 194. See also Microsoft
    Picture It!
multiple images on page, 164–167

N

negatives, 3–4
NiCad batteries, 19
night settings for flash, 55
NiMH batteries, 19
Nixvue digital albums, 26

O

Ofoto
    photo greeting cards from, 169
    Web site, 217
OfotoNow software, 85, 115
Olympus C-211 camera, 157
online photo services, 84–87, 169–174,
    216–217. See also specific photo services
    about, 169–170, 181
    Apple iPhoto, 86–87, 154, 171–174, 216
    Club Photo,188, 216
    Microsoft Picture It!, 85, 93, 111, 193, 217
    Ofoto, 169, 217
    PhotoAccess, 192, 217
    printing with, 169–174
    selecting, 183–185
    Snapfish, 170, 171, 217
    uploading and ordering photos to,
        170–171
    using Web pages of, 182–183
online resources, 215–217
opacity, 120–121
optical viewfinders, 30, 45
optical zoom, 15, 52
optimizing JPEG files, 107
organizing
    computer to store images, 64
    photos in folders, 72–73
    photos in iPhoto, 74–76

P

Paint Shop Pro. See Jasc Paint Shop Pro
panoramas, 194–197
paper, 160–164
    about types of, 160–162
    manufacturers' recommendations, 162
    printing surface of, 162
    special, 162–164
parallax, 30–31
PC Card, 62
PDAs, displaying photos on, 187–188
personal Web page for sharing photos,
    186–187
photo editors, 92–94
photo printers, 156
photo T-shirts, 191–192
PhotoAccess, 192, 217

photographs. *See also* composing photographs;
   prints; projects with photographs
     adding borders to, 134
     backing up online, 185
     captions for, 135
     cataloging software for, 75
     changing resolution and size, 132–133
     choosing file types, 95–96
     combining, 151–152, 213
     constraining proportions of, 133
     customizing computer desktop with,
       198–203
     deleting unwanted, 61, 177
     developing film, 3–4
     duplicating, 7
     editing guidelines for, 135
     hue, contrast, and brightness, 115–117
     increasing longevity of inkjet, 163
     knowing what to edit on, 109–111
     memory requirements for editing, 82–83
     moving from flash card to computer,
       65–66
     organizing, 72–73, 74–76
     preparing computer to store, 64
     previewing digital, 7
     recording images on VCR, 70, 74, 176–177
     resolution of, 5, 7
     saving, 70–72
     sound annotation of, 205
     space requirements for digital, 10
     stitching together, 194–197
     storing on CDs, 12
     transferring to computer, 64–68
     on T-shirts, 191–192
photography. *See also* digital photography
     advantages of film photography, 5–6
     history of, 2–3
     how digital cameras work, 4–5
     technology of photographic film, 3–4
PhotoImpact. *See* Ulead PhotoImpact
PhotoImpression. *See* ArcSoft PhotoImpression
Photo-Paint. *See* Corel Photo-Paint
PhotoPrinter, 166
Photoshop. *See* Adobe Photoshop
Photoshop Elements. *See* Adobe Photoshop
  Elements
PICT (picture) files, 100
Picture It!. *See* Microsoft Picture It!

Picture Package option (Photo Elements),
  165–166
picture T-shirts, 191–192
PictureGear Lite, 62
PixelNhance, 86–87
pixels. *See also* megapixels
    changing image resolution and
      resampling, 132–133
    defined, 4
    effect of resampling on, 131
    sampling and cloning, 124
PKZIP, 179
Playback mode, 60
PNG (Portable Network Graphics) files,
  100–101
PocketPoint, 188
Polaroid, 3
portraits
    composing, 41
    enhancing brightness of teeth, 146
    reducing wrinkles and blemishes on,
      144–148
    removing circles below eyes, 147–148
Portraits & Prints Template Maker, 166
ports
    FireWire, 12
    IEEE 1394, 12
    USB, 61–62
Preferences dialog box (iPhoto), 189
preparing photos for printing, 164–167
    chart of print sizes and suggested print
      resolution, 165
    printing several images on page, 164–167
previewing iPhoto albums, 173
Print Explosion Deluxe, 193
printers
    dither, 157
    general-purpose vs. photo, 155–157
    lubricating print head of, 160
    maintaining, 159–160
printing photographs, 153–174
    choosing paper for, 160–164
    at home, 153–154
    increasing longevity of inkjet prints, 163
    with inkjet printers and cartridges,
      154–160
    preparing images for print, 164–167
    professional printing services, 167–174
    self-service kiosks, 168

printing surface of paper, 162
prints
    changing resolution and size of, 130–131
    chart of sizes and suggested resolution, 165
    defined, 4
    increasing longevity of inkjet, 163
    multiple images on page, 164–167
    setting up for printing, 164–167
PrintSix, 166
PrintStation, 166
professional editing software, 94
professional printing services, 167–174.
    See also online photo services
    iPhoto printed albums, 173–174
    iPhoto prints, 171–173
    Kodak, 172
    local services, 168
    online services, 169–170
    overview, 167
    uploading and ordering photos with online, 170–171
professional-quality digital cameras
    costs of, 17
    resolution for, 14
progressive JPEG files, 107
projects with photographs, 191–205
    adding sound annotation to images, 205
    customizing computer desktop, 198–203
    documenting online sale items, 197–198
    photo greeting cards, 193–194
    photo panoramas, 194–197
    shooting movies with camera, 203–205
    T-shirts, 191–192
PSD file format, 101

Q

quality settings for JPEG files, 97, 105–107

R

RAM
    image editing and requirements for, 82–83
    requirements for digital photographs, 9–10
RAW files, 98–100
RAW Image Converter software, 99
recording photos on VCR, 70, 74, 176–177
red eye
    techniques for reducing, 53, 114

red-eye-reduction tools, 113–115
    tool changes eye color to gray, 212
reducing glare of flash, 54–55, 56
reflex cameras, 30
removing wrinkles and blemishes, 144–148
renaming
    photos to describe file content, 73
    transferred photos, 71
resampling
    changing image resolution and, 132–133
    effect of on pixels, 131
resolution
    changing display, 199
    changing image size and, 132–133
    changing print size and, 130–131
    chart of print sizes and suggested, 165
    choosing correct, 43–44
    cloning and image, 125
    dither, 157
    of film images, 5
    setting on camera, 44–45
retail stores, 18
Rule of Thirds, 34

S

Save As a Copy command, 103
Save As command, 103
Save As dialog box, 71, 104
saving
    files in JPEG format, 105–107
    files in TIFF format, 104–105
    original and edited copies of files, 103
    photos, 70–72
screen hood, 31
Screen Saver dialog box (iPhoto), 202
screensavers, 201–203
selecting online photo services, 183–185
selection tools, 112–113
self-timer/remote control function, 57
serial port connections, 62
setting camera features, 43–57
    exposure, 47–51
    flash, 52–56
    focus, 45–47
    resolution settings, 43–45
    self-timer/remote control, 57
    zoom, 51–52
setting up pictures, 28–29
Share button (iPhoto), 171

shareware
    defined, 79
    file compression software, 179
    GraphicConverter, 93–94
    iView MediaPro, 189–190
    printing, 166–167
    vs. commercial software, 79–80
sharing photos, 175–190
    digital slide shows, 188–190
    emailing images, 177–181
    with iPhoto online, 185–186
    on PDAs, 187–188
    on personal Web page, 186–187
    as printed photos or video output, 70, 74, 175–177
    selecting online services, 183–185
    using online photo services, 181–183
sharpening tools, 127–129
shooting
    against light, 36–38
    movies, 203–205
    objects in motion, 39–40
ShortCourses Web site, 216
shutter. *See also* exposure
    adjusting speed of, 38–39
    defined, 4
    setting speed for objects in motion, 39–40
    shooting without flash, 54–55
    shutter latency, 5
    shutter priority, 48–49
single lens reflex (SLR) camera, 30
SIT files, 179, 180
size
    changing image, 132–133
    changing print, 130–131
SmartMedia cards, 21
Snapfish photo services
    quality of, 169, 170
    samples of photos from, 154
    uploading photos to, 170–171
    Web site, 182–183, 217
software. *See also specific software by name*
    checking requirements for computer, 9
    checking tools for image editing in, 111
    choosing editing, 78–80
    drop-and-crop editing, 84–87
    file compression, 179–180

    freeware and shareware vs. commercial, 79–80
    image editors, 81, 87–92
    image-stitching, 196–197
    for photo displays on PDAs, 188
    photo editors, 92–94
    printing template shareware, 166–167
    selecting cataloging, 75
    types of editing, 80–82, 84
    USB compatibility of operating system, 10–11
sound annotation for images, 205
special printing paper, 162–164
SplashPhoto, 188
stitching, 196–197
storage capacity
    film vs. digital camera, 5–6
    reusing storage cards, 7
    space requirements for images, 10
    storing images on CDs, 12
storage cards
    buying extra, 25
    capacity of, 5–6
    card readers for, 22
    CompactFlash cards, 21
    downloading images from, 25–26
    Memory Sticks, 22
    overview, 20–21
    reusability of, 7
    showing images in digital frame, 176
    SmartMedia cards, 21
    Trouble reading, 209
storing and transferring photos, 59–76
    burning CD of original photos, 73–74
    connecting camera to computer, 61–64
    deleting unwanted shots, 61, 177
    organizing photos, 72–73, 74–76
    recording images on VCR, 70, 74, 176–177
    saving and renaming photos, 70–72
    selecting cataloging software, 75
    setting up computer folders to store images, 64
    subscriptions for online photo storage, 184
    transferring photos to computer, 64–68
    viewing images stored on camera, 60
    viewing transferred photos, 68–70

StuffIt, 179
StuffIt Expander for Windows, 179, 180
subscriptions for online photo storage, 184

T

TIFF (Tagged Image File Format) files
    advantages of saving files as, 71
    features of, 98
    saving files in, 104–105
tone, 138
transferring photos to computer, 64–68
    erasing flash card, 66–67
    with infrared connection, 66
    overview, 64–65
    renaming transferred photos, 71
    swapping flash cards, 67–68
    viewing transferred photos, 68–70
tripods, 24–25
troubleshooting
    camera, 207–209
    image editing, 211–213

U

Ulead PhotoImpact, 90–91, 128
uploading files and Internet connections, 182
USB (Universal Serial Bus) card readers, 22
USB PCI card, 62
USB ports
    about compatibility of software and, 9, 10–11
    adding to computers, 62
    connecting camera to computer with, 61–62

V

Variations dialog box (Photoshop Elements), 110
VCRs
    recording photos on, 74, 176–177
    viewing transferred photos via, 70
VCW VicMan Photo Editor, 88
video output of photos, 70, 74, 175–177
viewfinders
    optical, 30, 45
    reflex, 30
viewing
    images stored on camera, 60
    photos on computer, 68–69
    transferred photos on TV, 70
viewing mode, 60

W

Web sites
    configuring visitor access to Web albums, 183
    graphics formats suitable for, 100–101
    online resources on, 215–217
    personal Web pages, 186–187
white balance settings, 50–51
Windows. *See* Microsoft Windows
WinZip, 179
wrinkles and blemishes, 144–148

Y

Yahoo, 187

Z

zoom, 51–52
    focusing background images with, 32
    optical vs. digital, 15, 51–52